ON WRITING

Eudora Welty

On Writing

Introduction by Richard Bausch

THE MODERN LIBRARY

NEW YORK

The essays in this work were originally published in the following
journals: *The Atlantic Monthly, Critical Inquiry, South Atlantic Quarterly,
Southern Review*, and *The Virginia Quarterly Review*. They were
subsequently published in book form in *The Eye of the Story*
(Random House, Inc., 1978).

LIBRARY OF CONGRESS CATALOGING-IN-PUBLICATION DATA
Welty, Eudora, 1909–
On writing / Eudora Welty.
p.   cm.
ISBN 0-679-64270-6
1. Fiction—Authorship.   2. Fiction—Technique.   I. Title.
PN3355 .W375 2002
808.3—dc21
2002022340

Modern Library website address: www.modernlibrary.com

Printed in the United States of America on acid-free paper

2 4 6 8 9 7 5 3 1

EUDORA WELTY

Eudora Welty was born in Jackson, Mississippi, on April 13, 1909. Of her tranquil childhood she wrote: "I am a writer who came of a sheltered life. A sheltered life can be a daring life as well. For all serious daring starts from within." She studied at Mississippi State College for Women, the University of Wisconsin, and Columbia University, with the intention of pursuing a career in advertising, an idea abandoned in favor of writing after her stories began to be published regularly in the mid-1930s. The appearance of her work in *The New Yorker* and *The Atlantic Monthly* established a reputation that was furthered by the publication of her first story collection, *A Curtain of Green*, in 1941. After her college days she returned to Jackson, where she would live permanently.

Further stories were collected in *The Wide Net* (1943), *The Golden Apples* (1949), *The Bride of the Innisfallen* (1955), and a book of stories for children, *The Shoe Bird* (1964). Another collection, *Moon Lake*, appeared in 1980, as did *The*

Collected Stories. The novella *The Robber Bridegroom* was published in 1942 and was followed by other longer works of fiction: *Delta Wedding* (1946), *The Ponder Heart* (1954), and, after a hiatus of several years, *Losing Battles* (1970), which focused new attention on her work. Her next book, *The Optimist's Daughter* (1972), won the Pulitzer Prize. A collection of essays, *The Eye of the Story* (1978), was followed by the memoir *One Writer's Beginnings*, which in 1984 became an unexpected best-seller.

In addition to her work as a writer, Welty published a book of photographs, *One Time, One Place* (1971), recording her visual impressions of Mississippi in the early thirties. Two of her books, *The Ponder Heart* and *The Robber Bridegroom*, have been adapted for the stage.

Eudora Welty died on July 23, 2001, at the age of ninety-two.

Contents

INTRODUCTION

Richard Bausch

One evening not so long ago, I was present at a gathering in the Episcopal Church across from the Folger Shakespeare Library in Washington, D.C. It was late October, and there was a crispness in the air, the trees lining the avenues were all blazing with color. I was then a member of the PEN/Faulkner Board, and though the occasion was decidedly secular rather than religious, it was certainly spiritual: Miss Eudora Welty, then eighty-six years old, was going to read one of her stories.

Earlier, at the dinner which always precedes such events, she had told how a town librarian once approached her, wanting her to come speak. "What we'd like you to do," the librarian said, "is come tell us one of your stories in your own words." Miss Welty's eyes sparkled, relating this story, and there was no dismissal at all in her voice, no sense of the librarian as someone at whose expense the story was told. It was as if this were a tale of the kind of sweet innocence that a child might inspire, and even that isn't adequate as a depiction of the attitude: for Miss Welty was in fact delighted by it. One would almost say gladdened. There was something in her spirit that was always outward-aimed, and glad of human foible, and it is hard to express exactly how it shone forth: one simply knew it when one was in its presence.

At the Fellowship of Southern Writers Luncheon back in 1991, I plopped down next to her and stuck a fork into the chicken cordon-bleu that had been placed before me, and then realized that someone was saying a prayer for the gathering and that the whole audience, including people whom I knew quite well to be pagan, had heads bowed, hands folded. I couldn't get the fork out of the chicken, and so I sat back and put my head down, and waited. When the prayer was finished, Miss Eudora leaned over to me and murmured, "I believe it's already killed." I still think about the look of mischievous gladness in her eyes and I smile.

And now, years later, she was going to read her story "A Wide Net" to this large gathering, a packed church, people standing all along the walls and in back, and seated on the floor in the central aisle and across the front of the elevation that led to the altar behind her. There was a small table, with a book and a microphone on it, and one glass of water. She was so frail that she had to be helped across to the chair. She took her place, and the microphone was adjusted at the angle necessary to broadcast her thin, quiet voice, with the lilt of Mississippi in it, and its kindly tremor of humor and grace, and, well, goodness. Nothing less. She got comfortable in the chair, arranged herself, looked out at the throng, smiling, nodded slightly, waiting for the applause to die down. She opened the book, adjusted her glasses, looked at the page and waited a second, then began to read. The silence, as she spoke, and went on, was profound. No one coughed or cleared his throat; no one shifted weight or moved papers or fumbled with a purse—for that might have meant missing a word or phrase. The voice was so small, scarcely more than a murmur. When there were laughs—and she knew precisely where they all were, and took pleasure in them without making a show of it—she waited, patiently, until the silence returned, and then continued, in the same soft, warm tones, the voice of an intimate friend, telling you secrets you didn't know you knew.

Here, in the Modern Library, is this wonderful book, filled with all her best virtues as a writer and as a person. Rich with her great wisdom not only about the art she practiced so well all the years, but about life, and the intelligent living of it. Any student of literature would do well to study *On Writing,* because this book contains the words of a great practitioner of the art of fiction, spelling out the matters of her craft. But there is plenty for anyone interested in how to live, too. Here she is discussing place in fiction:

> There may come to be new places in our lives that are second spiritual homes—closer to us in some ways, perhaps, than our original homes. But the home tie is the blood tie.

That applies to her subject, but it also contains wisdom of its own, separate from the esthetic she's describing, or extending from it.

So this book on craft is of general interest, it seems to me. And even so, I expect that young writers of fiction will be carrying it around with them in the years to come. They ought to be, anyway.

Miss Welty uses her own work and the work of artists she admires from her wide reading to talk about the forms of fiction, and the application of these matters to the life we lead: there is an essay on the writing of stories, and another on analyzing fiction; there's one about the uses of place in the novel, and there's another about words themselves in the construction of a fictive world. Each essay contains windows into the mind and soul of Eudora Welty the reader, as well as the writer. Here she is discussing Virginia Woolf, D. H. Lawrence, and Chekhov:

> For Virginia Woolf . . . the senses mattered extremely, as we know; toward sex she was a critic. But the beauty and innovation of her writing are both due to the fact, it seems to this reader, that the imprisonment of life in the word was with her a concern of the intellect as much as it was with the senses. She uses her senses intellectually, while Lawrence, if this is not too easy to say, uses his intellect sensually. While Chekhov patiently builds up character, Lawrence furiously breaks down character. . . . Chekhov was exorcizing nothing, he simply showed it forth.

But as I have indicated, there is more than literary criticism here. Her essay "Must the Novelist Crusade?," written at the height of the civil rights crisis of the middle sixties, is fresh and burning with truth. In that essay, she confronts the evil of her time with toughness and compassion:

I believe there must be such a thing as sentimental hate. . . . I think the worst of it is that we are getting stuck in it. We are like trapped flies with our feet not in honey but in venom. It's not love that is the gluey emotion; it's hate. As far as writing goes, which is as far as living goes, this is a devastating emotion. It could kill us.

But she also addresses the notion that it is the novelist's duty to be a crusader:

. . . the zeal to reform, which quite properly inspires the editorial, has never done fiction much good. The exception occurs when it can rise to the intensity of satire, where it finds a better home in the poem or the drama. Large helpings of naïveté and self-esteem, which serve to refresh the crusader, only encumber the novelist. How unfair it is that when a novel is to be written, it is never enough to have our hearts in the right place! But good will all by itself can no more get a good novel written than it can paint in watercolor or sing Mozart.

The one thing most evident in all her criticism is good sense.

And that is what is so frequently lacking in the criticism of our day, the era that has been termed postmodern, and that I have elsewhere called post-sensical. It is an overly politicized era, in which the novelist is often faced with an unspoken but very clear expectation that he indeed crusade; that one must be about the business of engineering better human beings, and correcting social ills, or redressing old social grievances. Fictive art is seen in terms of its political utility, its quotient of moral outrage. Everything is politics, the professors tell us, and the writer is morally bound to expose this or that injustice. And in keeping with this mentality, writers who have gone before us are lifted or devalued by how well they can withstand the heresy-hunting party line: for instance, Joseph Conrad was an imperialist, according to this feature of the critical climate, and Faulkner was a racist.

Well, this little book is all one needs to face into the prevailing silliness. And if I may borrow the sense of a phrase from her old friend and peer William Maxwell, Eudora Welty's heart is like a lovely cottage with all the windows and doors wide open. She reminds us, wonderfully, that "Beauty is not a means, not a way of furthering a thing in the world. It is a result; it belongs to ordering, to form, to aftereffect."

That October evening, while she read "A Wide Net" to all those people, my mind wandered just for an instant: I had the thought that this is what true civilization really is; not the cities or the monuments or the statecraft or even the politics: but this. This slip of a lady, with barely the physical power to get around on her own unaided, holding a thousand others in thrall, threaded together on the silence by the force and power of her art, her being, her imagining.

—

RICHARD BAUSCH is the author of fourteen volumes of fiction, including *Selected Stories* (a Modern Library hardcover), and, most recently, *Hello to the Cannibals*.

To Kenneth Millar

ON WRITING

LOOKING AT SHORT STORIES

Looking at short stories as readers and writers together should be a companionable thing. And why not? Stories in their bardic and fairy-tale beginnings were *told,* the listeners—and judgers—all in a circle.

E. M. Forster, in *Aspects of the Novel,* described the great age of the narrative:

> Neanderthal man listened to stories, if one may judge by the shape of his skull. The primitive audience was an audience of shock-heads, gaping around the camp-fire, fatigued with contending against the mammoth or woolly-rhinoceros, and only kept awake by suspense. What would happen next? The novelist droned on, and as soon as the audience guessed what happened next, they either fell asleep or killed him.

That suspense is still with us, but it seems to me that now it exists as something shared. Reader and writer make it a double experience. It is part of the great thing in which they share most—pleasure. And it is certainly part of the strong natural curiosity which readers feel to varying degree and which writers feel to the most compelling degree as to how any one story ever gets told. The only way a writer can satisfy his own curiosity is to write it. And how different this already makes it from telling it! Suspense, pleasure, curiosity, all are bound up in the making of the written story.

Forster went on to distinguish between what Neanderthal man told, the narrative thread, and what the written story has made into an art, the plot. "The king died and then the queen died" is the narrative thread; "The king died and then the queen died of grief" is a plot. We have all come from asking What next? to asking Why? The word "which," of course, opened up everything, or as much of everything as the writer is able to handle.

To take a story:

Jack Potter, the town marshal of Yellow Sky, has gone to San Anton' and got married and is bringing his bride back in a Pullman as a dazzling surprise for his hometown. And while the train is on its way, back in Yellow Sky Scratchy Wilson gets drunk and turns loose with both hands. Everybody runs to cover: he has come to shoot up the town. "And his boots had red tops with gilded imprints, of the kind beloved in winter by little sledding boys on the hillsides of New England . . . The only sounds were his terrible invitations . . . He comfortably fusilladed the windows of his most intimate friend. The man was playing with the town; it was a toy for him." The train comes in, Scratchy and the marshal are face to face, and Potter says, "I ain't got a gun on me, Scratchy," and takes only a minute to make up his mind to be shot on his wedding day. "If you ain't got a gun, why ain't you got a gun?" "I ain't got a gun because I've just come from San Anton' with my wife. I'm married." "Married? Married? . . . Is this the lady?" "Yes; this is the lady." " 'Well,' said Wilson at last, slowly, I s'pose it's all off now.' He was not a student of chivalry; it was merely that in the presence of this condition he was a simple child of the earlier plains." He picked up his starboard revolver, and, placing both weapons in their holsters, he went away.

Two predicaments meet here, in Stephen Crane's "The Bride Comes to Yellow Sky." You might say they are magnetized toward each other—and collide. One is vanquished with neatness and absurdity; as he goes away, Scratchy's "feet made funnel-shaped tracks in the heavy sand." Here are the plainest equivalents of comedy, two situations in a construction simple as a seesaw, and not without a seesaw's kind of pleasure in reading; like Scratchy Wilson, Crane is playing with us here.

In Katherine Mansfield's "Miss Brill," there is only one character and a single situation; Miss Brill's action consists nearly altogether in sitting down—she goes out to sit in the park, returns to sit on her bed. There is no collision. Rather, the forces meeting in the public gardens have, at the story's end, passed through each other and come out at the other side; there has been not a collision, but a change—something more significant. This is because, although there is one small situation going on, a large, complex one is implied. Life itself corresponds to the part of Scratchy Wilson, so to speak. Not violent life, merely life in a park on Sunday afternoon in Paris. All that it usually does for Miss Brill is promenade, yet, life being life, it does finally threaten. How much more deadly to such a lady than a flourished pistol is a remark overheard about herself. Reality comes to leer at her from a pleasant place, and she has not come prepared to bear it. And so she, who in her innocence could spare even pity for this world—pity, the spectator's emotion—is defeated. A word is spoken and the blow falls and Miss Brill retires, ridiculously easy to mow down, as the man with the pistols was easy to stare down in "Yellow Sky" for comedy's sake. But Miss Brill was from the first defenseless and on the losing side; her defeat is the deeper for it and one feels sure it is for always. So this story, instead of being a simple situation, is an impression of a situation, and tells more for being so.

Looking at these two stories by way of their plots in skeleton, we can't help but notice something: their plots are not unlike. "The Bride Comes to Yellow Sky" is its more unpretentious form, "Miss Brill" shows an interesting variation. It is a plot with two sides, or two halves, or two opposites, or two states of mind or feeling side by side; even one such in repeat would be a form of this. The plot is, of course, life *versus* death, which includes nearly every story in the world.

It could be said equally well that most stories (and novels too) have plots of the errand of search. An idea this pervasive simply pervades life, and the generality that could include in one quick list "The Bear," "The Jolly Corner," "The Short Happy Life of Francis Macomber" and "Araby" doesn't tell us really anything.

And so, plainly, we must distinguish plots not by their skeletons but by their full bodies; for they are embodiments, little worlds. Here is another: let us try to distinguish it as if it were literally a little world, and spinning closely now into our vision.

Now, the first thing we notice about this story is that we can't really see its solid outlines—it seems bathed in something of its own. It is wrapped in an atmosphere. This is what makes it shine, perhaps, as well as what obscures, at first glance, its plain real shape.

We are bearing in mind that the atmosphere in a story may be not the least of its glories, and also the fact that it may give a first impression that will prove contrary to what lies under it. Some action stories fling off the brightest clouds of obscuring and dazzling light, like ours here. Penetrate that atmosphere and the object may show quite dark within, for all its clouds of speed, those primary colors of red and yellow and blue. It looks like one of Ernest Hemingway's stories, and it is.

A story behaves, it goes through motions—that's part of it. Some stories leave a train of light behind them, meteorlike, so that much later than they strike our eyes we may see their meaning like an aftereffect. And Faulkner's seem not meteors but comets; they have a course of their own that brings them around more than once; they reappear in their own time in the sense that they reiterate their meaning and show a whole further story over and beyond their single significance.

If we have thought of Hemingway's stories as being bare and solid as billiard balls, so scrupulously cleaned of adjectives, of every unneeded word, as they are, of being plain throughout as a verb is plain, we may come to think twice about it, from our stargazer distance. The atmosphere that cloaks D. H. Lawrence's stories is of sensation, which is pure but thick cover, a cloak of self-illuminating air, but the atmosphere that surrounds Hemingway's is just as thick and to some readers less illuminating. Action can indeed be inscrutable, more so than sensation can. It can be just as voluptuous, too, just as vaporous, and, as I am able to see it, much more desperately concealing.

In one of Hemingway's early stories, "Indian Camp," Nick goes with his father, a doctor, to see a sick Indian woman. She is suffering in labor and the doctor operates on her without an anaesthetic. In the bunk above her head, her husband lies with a sore foot. After the operation is over and the child successfuly born, the husband is found to have slit his throat because he had not been able to bear his wife's suffering. Nick asks, "Is dying hard, Daddy?" "No, I think it's pretty easy," his father says.

Is this still a red and blue world? I see it as dark as night. Not that it is obscure; rather, it's opaque. Action can be radiant, but in this writer who has action to burn, it is not. The stories are opaque by reason of his intention, which is to moralize. We are to be taught by Hemingway, who is instructive by method, that the world is dangerous and full of fear, and that there is a way we had better be. There is nothing for it but, with bravery, to observe the ritual. And so action can step in front of reality just as surely and with more agility than even sentimentality can. Our belligerent planet Mars has an unknown and unrevealed heart.

Nevertheless, this is not where we stop seeing. For what comes of this, his method? In a painting by Goya, who himself used light, action and morality dramatically, of course, the bullring and the great turbulent wall of spectators are cut in diagonal halves by a great shadow of afternoon (unless you see it as the dark sliced away by the clear, golden light): half the action revealed and half hidden in dense, clotting shade. It's like this in Hemingway's plots. And it seems to be the halving that increases the story.

One power of his, his famous use of dialogue, derives as well from the fact that something is broken in two; language slips, meets a barrier, a shadow is inserted between the speakers. It is an obscuring and at the same time a revealing way to write dialogue, and only great skill can manage it—and make us aware at the same time that communication of a limited kind is now going on as best it can.

As we now see Hemingway's story, not transparent, not radiant, but lit from outside the story, from a moral source, we see that light's true nature: it is a spotlight. And his stories are all taking place as entirely in the present as plays we watch being acted on the stage. Pasts and futures are among the things his characters have not. Outside this light, they are nothing.

Clearly, the fact that stories have plots in common is of no more account than that many people have blue eyes. Plots are, indeed, what the story writer sees with, and so do we as we read. The plot is the Why. Why? is asked and replied to at various depths; the fishes in the sea are bigger the deeper we go. To learn that character is a more awe-inspiring fish and (in a short story, though not, I think, in a novel) one some degrees deeper down than situation, we have only to read Chekhov. What constitutes the reality of his characters is what they reveal to us. And the possibility that they may indeed reveal everything is what makes fictional characters differ so greatly from us in real life; yet isn't it strange that they don't really *seem* to differ? This is one clue to the extraordinary magnitude of character in fiction. Characters in the plot connect us with the vastness of our secret life, which is endlessly explorable. This is their role. What happens to them is what they have been put here to show.

In his story "The Darling," the darling's first husband, the theatre manager, dies suddenly *because* of the darling's sweet passivity; this is the causality of fiction. In everyday or real life he might have held on to his health for years. But under Chekhov's hand he is living and dying in dependence on, and in revelation of, Olenka's character. He can only last a page and a half. Only by force of the story's circumstance is he here at all; Olenka took him up to begin with because he lived next door.

Olenka listened to Kukin with silent gravity, and sometimes tears came into her eyes. In the end his misfortunes touched her; she grew to love him. He was a small thin man, with a yellow face; as he talked his mouth worked on one side, and there was always an expression of despair on his face; yet he aroused a deep and genuine affection in her. She was always fond of someone, and could not exist without loving. In earlier days she had loved her papa, who now sat in a darkened room, breathing with difficulty; she had loved her aunt, who used to come every other year from Bryansk; and before that, when she was at school, she had loved her French master. She was a gentle, soft-hearted, compassionate girl, with mild, tender eyes and very good health. At the sight of her full rosy cheeks, her soft white neck with a little dark mole on it, and the kind, naïve smile, which came into her face when she listened to anything pleasant, men thought, "Yes, not half bad," and smiled too, while lady-visitors could not refrain from seizing her hand in the middle of a conversation, exclaiming in a gush of delight, "You darling!"

Kukin proposes and they are married.

> And when he had a closer view of her neck and her plump, fine shoulders, he threw up his hand and said "You darling!" . . . And what Kukin said about the the-atre and the actors she repeated. Like him she despised the public for their ignorance and indifference to art; she took part in the rehearsals, she corrected the actors, she kept an eye on the behavior of the musicians, and when there was an unfavorable notice in the local paper, she shed tears, and then went to the editor's office to set things right . . .

And when Kukin dies, Olenka's cry of heartbreak is this: "Vanitchka, my precious, my darling! Why did I ever meet you! Why did I know you and love you! Your poor broken-hearted Olenka is all alone without you!"

With variations the pattern is repeated, and we are made to feel it as plot, aware of its clear open stress, the variations all springing from Chekhov's boundless and minute perception of character. The timber-merchant, an-other neighbor, is the one who walks home from the fu-neral with Olenka. The outcome follows tenderly, is only natural. After three days, he calls. "He did not stay long, only about ten minutes, and he did not say much, but when he left, Olenka loved him—loved him so much that she lay awake all night in a perfect fever."

Olenka and Pustovalov get along very well together when they are married.

"Timber gets dearer every year; the price rises twenty per cent," she would say to her customers and friends . . . "And the freight!" she would add, covering her cheeks with her hands in horror, "the freight!" . . . It seemed to her that she had been in the timber trade for ages and ages; and that the most important and necessary thing in life was timber; and there was something intimate and touching to her in the very sound of words such as "post," "beam," "pole," "batten," "lath," "plank," and the like.

Even in her dreams Olenka is in the timber business, dreaming of "perfect mountains of planks and boards," and cries out in her sleep, so that Pustovalov says to her tenderly, "Olenka, what's the matter, darling? Cross yourself!" But the timber merchant inevitably goes out in the timber yard one day without his cap on; he catches cold and dies, to leave Olenka a widow once more. "I've nobody, now you've left me, my darling," she sobs after the funeral. "How can I live without you?"

And the timber merchant is succeeded by a veterinary surgeon—who gets transferred to Siberia. But the plot is not repetition—it is direction. The love which Olenka bears to whatever is nearest her reaches its final and, we discover, its truest mold in maternalism: for there it is most naturally innocent of anything but formless, thoughtless, blameless *embracing;* the true innocence is in never perceiving. Only mother love could endure in a pursuit of such blind regard, caring so little for the reality of either life involved so long as love wraps them together, Chekhov tells us—unpretentiously, as he tells everything, and with the simplest of concluding episodes. Olenka's character is seen purely then for what it is: limpid reflection, mindless and purposeless regard, love that falls like the sun and rain on all alike, vacant when there is nothing to reflect.

We know this because, before her final chance to love, Olenka is shown to us truly alone:

> [She] got thinner and plainer; and when people met her in the street they did not look at her as they used to, and did not smile to her; evidently her best years were over and left behind, and now a new sort of life had begun for her, which did not bear thinking about . . . And what was worst of all, she had no opinions of any sort. She saw the objects about her and understood what she saw, but could not form any opinions about them, and did not know what to talk about. And how awful it is not to have any opinions! She wanted a love that would absorb her whole being, her whole soul and reason—that would give her ideas and an object in life, and would warm her old blood.

The answer is Sasha, the ten-year-old son of the veterinary surgeon, an unexpected blessing from Siberia—a schoolchild. The veterinarian has another wife now, but this no longer matters. "Olenka, with arms akimbo, walked about the yard giving directions. Her face was beaming, and she was brisk and alert, as though she had waked from a long sleep . . ." "An island is a piece of land entirely surrounded by water," Sasha reads aloud. " 'An island is a piece of land,' she repeated, and this was the first opinion to which she gave utterance with positive conviction, after so many years of silence and dearth of ideas." She would follow Sasha halfway to school, until he told her to go back.

She would go to bed thinking blissfully of Sasha, "who lay sound asleep in the next room, sometimes crying out in his sleep, 'I'll give it to you! Get away! Shut up!' "

The darling herself *is* the story; all else is sacrificed to her; deaths and departures are perfunctory and to be expected. The last words of the story are the child's and a protest, but they are delivered in sleep, as indeed protest to the darlings of this world will always be—out of inward and silent rebellion alone, as this master makes plain.

It is when the plot, whatever it is, is nearest to becoming the same thing on the outside as it is deep inside, that it is purest. When it is identifiable in every motion and progression of its own with the motions and progressions of the story's feeling and its intensity, then this is plot put to its highest use.

This brings us to another story.

One evening, March was standing with her back to the sunset, her gun under her arm, her hair pushed up under her cap. She was half watching, half musing. It was her constant state. Her eyes were keen and observant, but her inner mind took no notice of what she saw. She was always lapsing into this odd, rapt state, her mouth rather screwed up. It was a question whether she was there, actually, consciously present, or not ... What was she thinking about? Heaven knows. Her consciousness was, as it were, held back.

She lowered her eyes and suddenly saw the fox. He was looking up at her. His chin was pressed down, and his eyes were looking up. They met her eyes. And he knew her. She was spellbound—she knew he knew her. So he looked into her eyes, and her soul failed her. He knew her, he was not daunted.

She struggled, confusedly she came to herself, and saw him making off, with slow leaps over some fallen boughs, slow, impudent jumps. Then he glanced over his shoulder, and ran smoothly away. She saw his brush held smooth like a feather, she saw his white buttocks twinkle. And he was gone, softly, soft as the wind.

In this long story by D. H. Lawrence, "The Fox," March and Banford, two girls, run a chicken farm by themselves in the country. As we see, it has its fox. They struggle against his encroachments, also against poverty and the elements, until a young soldier on leave, Henry, appears in the door one night. He has a vague story about his grandfather's once having lived here. March, the hunter and the man of the place, has not, as you know, shot the fox. But she has been, to use her word to herself, "impressed" by him. And here is Henry:

He had a ruddy, roundish face, with fairish hair, rather long, flattened to his forehead with sweat. His eyes were blue, and very bright and sharp. On his cheeks, on the fresh ruddy skin, were fine fine hairs like a down, but sharper. It gave him a slightly glistening look . . . He stooped, thrusting his head forward . . . He stared brightly, very keenly, from girl to girl, particularly at March, who stood pale, with great dilated eyes. She still had the gun in her hand. Behind her, Banford, clinging to the sofa arm, was shrinking away, with half-averted head.

So Henry, not on any account because of his cock-and-bull story, is taken in to spend his leave here. As expected by all, he proves himself a calculating, willful being, and proposes to marry March.

He scarcely admitted his intention to himself. He kept it as a secret even from himself . . . He would have to go gently . . . It's no good walking out into the forest and saying to the deer: "Please fall to my gun." No, it is a slow, subtle battle . . . It is not so much what you *do*, when you go out hunting, as how you *feel*. You have to be subtle and cunning, and absolutely, fatally ready . . . It is a subtle, profound battle of wills, which takes place in the invisible. And it is a battle never finished till your bullet goes home . . . It is your own *will* which carries the bullet into the heart of your quarry . . . And it was as a young hunter that he wanted to bring down March as his quarry, to make her his wife.

Dreams occur, the fox prowls, March and Banford suffer and argue while Henry, prowling, exerts and practices his will: the farm's fox is disposed of by him.

Here we are at the heart of this story: One night,

March dreamed vividly. She dreamed she heard a singing outside, which she could not understand, singing that roamed round the house, in the fields and in the darkness. It moved her so, that she felt she must weep. She went out, and suddenly she knew it was the fox singing. He was very yellow and bright, like corn. She went nearer to him, but he ran away and ceased singing. He seemed near, and she wanted to touch him. She stretched out her hand, but suddenly he bit her wrist, and at the same instant, as she drew back, the fox, turning round to bound away, whisked his brush across her face, and it seemed his brush was on fire, for it seared and burned her mouth with a great pain. She awoke with the pain of it, and lay trembling as if she were really seared.

Banford, the sensitive one, dies when Henry deliberately fells a tree her way, and Henry and March marry and are to be unhappy and embattled forever after.

And now, in Lawrence's work, what of his extraordinary characters? Are they real, recognizable, neat men and women? Would you know them if you saw them? Not even, I think, if they began to speak on the street as they speak in his stories, in the very words—they would appear as deranged people. And for this there is the most reliable of reasons: Lawrence's characters don't really speak their words, and they're not walking about on the street. They are playing like fountains or radiating like the moon or storming like the sea, or their silence is the silence of wicked rocks. It is borne home to us that Lawrence is writing of human relationships on earth in terms of his own heaven and hell, and on these terms plot and characters are alike sacrificed to something: that which Lawrence passionately believes to transcend both and which is known and found directly through the senses. It is the world of the senses that Lawrence writes in. He almost literally writes from within it. He is first wonderful at making a story world, a place, and then wonderful again when he inhabits it with six characters, the five senses and sex. And the plot is by necessity a symbolic one. We know straight from the start in "The Fox" that every point in the story is to be made *subjectively*. "He knew her. And she knew he knew her." And we know she knew he knew her: this by his almost super-normal appeal to, and approach by way of, what can be seen, felt and heard. What has made this story strange is also what empowers us to understand it. It is hypnotic. Human relationships in his stories are made forces so strong that *what* they are (and what you and I should perhaps find indescribable) is simply, when we read him, accepted without question.

It is characteristic of Lawrence that in describing the relationship between the two women, March and Banford, which is outwardly unconventional, he is stating perfectly clearly within his story's terms the conventional separation at work in the two halves of the personality—the conscious and the unconscious, or the will and the passive susceptibility, what is "ready" and what is submerged. March and Banford may well be the two halves of one woman, of woman herself in the presence of the male will. Lawrence prosecutes his case with the persistence of a lawyer, with the mowing down of any dissent that the prophet is allowed to practice. But what moves, convinces, persuades us, all the same, is, so to speak, the odor of the fox—for the senses, the poetic world that lies far deeper than these shafts of argument or preaching really go, work Lawrence's spell.

For Virginia Woolf in her stories the senses mattered extremely, as we know; toward sex she was a critic. But the beauty and the innovation of her writing are both due to the fact, it seems to this reader, that the imprisonment of life in the word was with her a concern of the intellect as much as it was with the senses. She uses her senses intellectually, while Lawrence, if this is not too easy to say, uses his intellect sensually. While Chekhov patiently builds up character, Lawrence furiously breaks down character. It doesn't need fiction writers to tell us that opposite things are very often done in getting at the truth. But it was Lawrence who was like the True Princess, who felt that beneath forty featherbeds there was a pea. Lawrence was as sensitive to falsity as the True Princess was to the pea, and he was just as sure to proclaim the injury. He quarrels with us terribly, of course, because it matters to him, in getting his story to the way he wants it, to quarrel.

Those who write with cruelty, and Lawrence is one, may not be lacking in compassion but stand in need to write in exorcisement. Chekhov was exorcising nothing, he simply showed it forth. He does not perhaps put his own feelings above life. Lawrence in his stories protests the world, and at the same time he gives the world an almost unbearable wonder and beauty.

His stories may at times remind you of some kind of tropical birds, that are in structure all but awkward—for what is symbolic has a very hard time if it must be at all on the ground; but then when they take wing, as they do, the miracle occurs. For Lawrence is an artist: his birds fly. Outrageousness itself is put to use, along with all that is felicitous. The bird in its flight is in superb command, our eyes are almost put out by iridescence. The phoenix really was his bird.

So much for "The Fox." "The Bear" begins:

There was a man and a dog too this time. Two beasts, counting Old Ben the bear, and two men, counting Boon Hogganbeck, in whom some of the same blood

ran which ran in Sam Fathers, even though Boon's was a
plebeian strain of it and in only Sam and Old Ben and
the mongrel Lion was taintless and incorruptible.

And we're in a different world. There is a world outside,
which we're expected to be acquainted with in its several
stratifications, to which our inner world communicates and
to which it answers. The blood in this story may not be
conscious or unconscious, but it can be *tainted*—that is, it
can be considered in its relation to action, to opinion, to
life going on outside. Blood can be plebeian, mongrel,
taintless, incorruptible in one sentence of William Faulkner's, whereas in all of Lawrence it is one thing, the abode
of the unconscious.

You will remember that this is a hunting story. A boy has
known always of a great bear in the hunting country he was
born into; encounters the bear after his initiation into the
wilderness, and does not kill him; but at last, years later,
with a beast that is trained to be his match (the mongrel,
Lion), the fatal encounter takes place, and bear, dog and
old pure-blooded Indian all die of it.

We see at once as we read that this narrative has the
quality of happening, and the blood of inheriting; the story
indeed has signs of having so much to do with the outer
world that it can happen, and has happened, more than
once. In one respect, this story is a sample of that happening which is continuous, indigenous to the time and the
place and the human element in and through which it happens.

Ike McCaslin, in whose experience at various stages we
are told the story,

realized later that it had begun long before that. It had already begun on that day when he first wrote his age in two ciphers and his cousin McCaslin brought him for the first time to the camp, the big woods, to earn for himself from the wilderness the name and state of hunter provided he in his turn were humble and enduring enough.

Humble and enduring—qualities that apply to our relationship with the world.

He had already inherited then, without ever having seen it, the big old bear with one trap-ruined foot that in an area of almost a hundred square miles had earned for himself a name, a definite designation like a living man—the long legend of corncribs broken down and rifled, of shoats and grown pigs and even calves carried bodily into the woods and devoured, and traps and deadfalls overthrown and dogs mangled and slain, and shotgun and even rifle shots delivered at pointblank range yet with no more effect than so many peas blown through a tube by a child—a corridor of wreckage and destruction beginning back before the boy was born, through which sped, not fast but rather with the ruthless and irresistible deliberation of a locomotive, the shaggy tremendous shape. It ran in his knowledge before he ever saw it. It loomed and towered in his dreams before he ever saw the unaxed woods where it left its crooked print, shaggy, tremendous, red-eyed, not malevolent but just big, too big for the dogs which tried to bay it, for the horses which tried to ride it, for the men and the bullets they fired into it; too big for the very country which was its constricting scope.

See the outer edges of this bear becoming abstract—but this bear is not the fox. "It was as if the boy had already divined what his senses and intellect had not encompassed yet . . ."

For this bear belongs to the world, the world of experience:

> that doomed wilderness whose edges were being constantly and punily gnawed at by men with plows and axes who feared it because it was wilderness, men myriad and nameless even to one another in the land where the old bear earned a name, and through which ran not even a mortal beast but an anachronism indomitable and invincible out of an old, dead time, a phantom, epitome and apotheosis of the old, wild life which the little puny humans swarmed and hacked at in a fury of abhorrence and fear, like pygmies about the ankles of a drowsing elephant;—the old bear, solitary, indomitable, and alone; widowered, childless, and absolved of mortality—old Priam, reft of his old wife, and outliving all his sons.

Experience in the world is the very thread this story is put together with. Here is the footprint:

> Then, standing beside Sam in the thick great gloom of ancient wood and the winter's dying afternoon, he looked quietly down at the rotted log scored and gutted with claw marks and, in the wet earth beside it, the print

of the enormous warped two-toed foot ... For the first time he realized that the bear which had run in his listening and loomed in his dreams since before he could remember, and which therefore must have existed in the listening and the dreams of his cousin and Major de Spain and even old General Compson before they began to remember in their turn, was a mortal animal and that they had departed for the camp each November with no actual intention of slaying it, not because it could not be slain but because so far they had no actual hope of being able to.

Faulkner achieves the startling reality and nearness of the outside world by alternately dilating reality to the reach of abstraction and bringing it home with a footprint. It is reality that not only *is*, but *looms*—and this not just one time to one character, but over and over, with an insistent quality.

There are several encounters between Ike McCaslin and the bear. The final one is a death struggle when the bear is

on its hind feet, its back against a tree while the bellowing hounds swirled around it and once more Lion [the mongrel dog that is his match] drove in, leaping clear of the ground. This time the bear didn't strike him down. It caught the dog in both arms, almost loverlike, and they both went down.

There is a terrible fight, Lion clings to the bear's throat and the bear tears at Lion's body and wounds him mortally, but Lion will not let go. Boon, Lion's trainer who loves him, when Lion is clawed, runs toward them, a knife in his hand. He flings himself astride the bear and the knife falls.

> It fell just once ... The bear then surged erect, raising with it the man and the dog too, and turned and still carrying the man and the dog it took two or three steps towards the woods on its hind feet as a man would have walked and crashed down. It didn't collapse, crumple. It fell all of a piece, as a tree falls, so that all three of them, man, dog and bear, seemed to bounce once.

The bear and the dog die of this, and so does Sam Fathers, the Indian, who is found lying motionless face down in the trampled mud when it's all over: not a mark on him, "he just quit." The bodies of the bear and Sam, open-eyed, teeth bared, brown—childless, kinless, peopleless—are stretched out alike.

"The Bear" ends with the death of three and a falling tree, as, you remember, "The Fox" ended—if you count the life-in-death of March and Henry as one death shared. The tree in Faulkner's story, along with the dying bear and his burden of victim and killer, is a wilderness falling. The fox is a denizen of the inner world, purely. The bear is, equally purely, of the outer world—not simply the material, three-dimensional outer world, which is good enough, but the measureless outer world of experience, the knowing and sentient past, the wisdom of Time and Place. Both bear and fox are vanquished by acts of the destructive will of man's aggression. But Faulkner's battles, taking place in an ever-present physical territory which now and again is also some projected country of the spirit, are conscious battles. Faulkner deals with such aspects of the human being as dignity and glory and corruptibility and incorruptibility and ridicule and defeat and pride and endurance—especially endurance, a word that might as well be in Cherokee to Lawrence. Lawrence's battles are won and lost in the "blood consciousness." It's as if the two worlds of Faulkner and Lawrence were, here, the inside-out of each other.

Faulkner seems to me, rather than an intuitive writer, a divining one. And his stories seem to race with time, race with the world, in an indirect ratio, perhaps, to the length of his sentences. The sixteen-thousand-word sentence in "The Bear" races like a dinosaur across the early fields of time. It runs along with a strange quality of seeming all to happen at once. It makes us realize once again that prose is a structure in its every part, that the imagination is engineered when we write. A sentence may be in as perfect control as a church or a bridge.

"The Bear" is an apocalyptic story of the end of the wilderness. It ends with the senseless clang on clang of a man idiotically pounding pieces of his broken gun together while in the isolated gum tree over his head forty or fifty squirrels are running frantically round and round. It signifies, for one thing, the arrival of the machine age and the squealing treadmill. This story encompasses past and future, all the past of the land from Indian times on to now. It has towering heroic figures, wilderness figures, symbolic figures; and through the hunter—whom we see in the present, in boyhood, the past, the future, in ancestry (in the ledgers and memories and paraphernalia of the place)— we are aware in every happening of its power to happen again, over and over; we are aware of the whole world of the wilderness, the whole history of Mississippi.

For in "The Bear," the structure of time is constantly in danger of being ripped away, torn down by the author; the *whole* time bulges, tries to get into the present-time of the story. This dilation in time sense and intractability in space sense, the whole surface of the story, has of itself a kind of looming quality, a portentousness. Like the skin of a balloon, time and space are stretched to hold more and more, while the story still holds it as long as it can, and in both form and function it dangerously increases.

And in Part Four of this long story the flimsy partition that keeps the story-time apart from whole time is allowed to fly away entirely. So the entire history of the land and a people crowds into a chapter whose expansion, in sentence and paragraph, is almost outrageous to the eye alone. Time and space have been too well invoked, and they tear through the story running backward and forward, up and down and around, like a pack of beasts themselves out of the world's wilderness. And this is the beauty of the story. Its self-destruction, self-immolation, is the way the story transcends all it might have been had it stayed intact and properly nailed together. There is its wonder.

Of course, such transcending might belong to some subjects and to other subjects it would bring foolishness. In the case of "The Bear" we can assume that to Faulkner the escapement of wild time and place seemed one attribute of the thing he was writing about—the lost attribute, implicit in it, and supplied now, in his story. In letting time and place out of the box he was not, by any standards but our ordinary ones, being reckless. By his own, he was being true, faithful to his composition of the story at hand. There is no other integrity.

———

We've observed how a story's great emphasis may fall on any of the things that make it up—on character, on plot, on its physical or moral world, in sensory or symbolic form. Now we may venture to say that it's this *ordering* of his story that is closest to the writer behind the writing, and that it's our perception of this ordering that gives us our nearest understanding of him.

And we have observed that the finest story writers seem to be in one sense obstructionists. As if they held back their own best interests—or what would be in another writer their best interests. It's a strange thing. And what is stranger is that if we look for the source of the deepest pleasure we receive from a writer, how often do we not find that it seems to be connected with this very obstruction.

The fact is, apparently, that in pressing to our source of pleasure we have entered into another world. We are speaking of beauty. And beauty is not a blatant or promiscuous or obvious quality; indeed, it is associated with reticence, with stubbornness, of a number of kinds. It arises somehow from a desire not to comply with what may be expected, but to act inevitably, as long as some human truth is in sight, whatever that inevitability may call for. Beauty is not a means, not a way of furthering a thing in the world. It is a result; it belongs to ordering, to form, to aftereffect.

Two qualities that cannot be imitated in this life, beauty and sensitivity, may in fiction's making be related to each other. But, reading and writing, we can only strive for one. Sensitivity in ourselves. And then beauty we may know, when we see it.

I think it ought to be said that a fiction writer can try anything. He has tried a great deal, but presumably not everything. The possibilities are endless because the stirring of the imagination never rests, and because we can never stop trying to make feeling felt.

So we know what will most pertinently describe the writing of our future too. Not rules, not esthetics, not problems and their solutions: not rules so long as there is imagination; not esthetics until after there is passion; not even problems that will always rise again and again for the honest writer. For at the other end of the writing is the reader. There is sure to be somewhere the reader, who is a user himself of imagination and thought, who knows, perhaps, as much about the need of communication as the writer.

Reader and writer, we wish each other well. Don't we want and don't we understand the same thing? A story of beauty and passion, some fresh approximation of human truth?

1949

WRITING AND ANALYZING

A STORY

Writers are often asked to give their own analysis of some story they have published. I never saw, as reader or writer, that a finished story stood in need of any more from the author: for better or worse, there the story is. There is also the question of whether or not the author could provide the sort of analysis asked for. Story writing and critical analysis are indeed separate gifts, like spelling and playing the flute, and the same writer proficient in both has been doubly endowed. But even he can't rise and do both at the same time.

To me as a story writer, generalizations about writing come tardily and uneasily, and I would limit them, if I were wise, by saying that any conclusions I feel confidence in are stuck to the particular story, part of the animal. The most trustworthy lesson I've learned from work so far is the simple one that the writing of each story is sure to open up a different prospect and pose a new problem; and that no past story bears recognizably on a new one or gives any promise of help, even if the writing mind had room for help and the wish that it would come. Help offered from outside the frame of the story would be itself an intrusion.

It's hard for me to believe that a writer's stories, taken in their whole, are written in any typical, predictable, systematically developing, or even chronological way—for all that a serious writer's stories are ultimately, to any reader, so clearly identifiable as his. Each story, it seems to me, thrives in the course of being written only as long as it seems to have a life of its own.

Yet it may become clear to a writer in retrospect (or so it did to me, although I may have been simply tardy to see it) that his stories have repeated themselves in shadowy ways, that they have returned and may return in future too—in variations—to certain themes. They may be following, in their own development, some pattern that's been very early laid down. Of course, such a pattern is subjective in nature; it may lie too deep to be consciously recognized until a cycle of stories and the actions of time have raised it to view. All the same, it is a pattern of which a new story is not another copy but a fresh attempt made in its own full-bodied right and out of its own impulse, with its own pressure, and its own needs of fulfillment.

It seems likely that all of one writer's stories do tend to spring from the same source within him. However they differ in theme or approach, however they vary in mood or fluctuate in their strength, their power to reach the mind or heart, all of one writer's stories carry their signature because of the one impulse most characteristic of his own gift—to praise, to love, to call up into view. But then, what countless stories by what countless authors share a common source! For the source of the short story is usually lyrical. And all writers speak from, and speak to, emotions eternally the same in all of us: love, pity, terror do not show favorites or leave any of us out.

The tracking down of a story might do well to start not in the subjective country but in the world itself. What in this world leads back most directly, makes the clearest connection to these emotions? What is the pull on the line? For some outside signal has startled or moved the story-writing mind to complicity: some certain irresistible, alarming (pleasurable or disturbing), magnetic person, place or thing. The outside world and the writer's response to it, the story's quotients, are always different, always differing in the combining; they are always—or so it seems to me—most intimately connected with each other.

This living connection is one that by its nature is not very open to generalization or discoverable by the ordinary scrutinies of analysis. Never mind; for its existence is, for any purpose but that of the working writer, of little importance to the story itself. It is of merely personal importance. But it is of extraordinary, if temporary, use to the writer for the particular story. Keeping this connection close is a writer's testing device along the way, flexible, delicate, precise, a means of guidance. I would rather submit a story to the test of its outside world, to show what it was doing and how it went about it, than to the method of critical analysis which would pick the story up by its heels (as if it had swallowed a button) to examine the writing process as analysis in reverse, as though a story—or any system of feeling—could be more accessible to understanding for being hung upside down.

It is not from criticism but from this world that stories come in the beginning; their origins are living reference plain to the writer's eye, even though to his eye alone. The writer's mind and heart, where all this exterior is continually *becoming* something—the moral, the passionate, the poetic, hence the *shaping* idea—can't be mapped and plotted. (Would this help—any more than a map hung on the wall changes the world?) It's the form it takes when it comes out the other side, of course, that gives a story something unique—its life. The story, in the way it has arrived at what it is on the page, has been something learned, by dint of the story's challenge and the work that rises to meet it—a process as uncharted for the writer as if it had never been attempted before.

Since analysis has to travel backward, the path it goes is an ever-narrowing one, whose goal is the vanishing point, beyond which only "influences" lie. But the writer of the story, bound in the opposite direction, works into the open. The choices multiply, become more complicated and with more hanging on them, as with everything else that has a life and moves. "This story promises me fear and joy and so I write it" has been the writer's beginning. The critic, coming to the end of his trail, may call out the starting point he's found, but the writer knew his starting point first and for what it was—the jumping-off place. And all along, the character of the choices—the critic's decisions and the writer's—is wholly different. I think that the writer's outbound choices were to him the *believable* ones, not necessarily defensible on other grounds; impelled, not subject to scheme but to feeling; that they came with an arrow inside them. They have been *fiction's* choices: one-way and fateful; strict as art, obliged as feeling, powerful in their authenticity.

The story and its analysis are not mirror-opposites of each other. They are not reflections, either one. Criticism indeed is an art, as a story is, but only the story is to some degree a vision; there is no explanation outside fiction for what its writer is learning to do. The simplest-appearing work may have been brought off (when it does not fail) on the sharp edge of experiment, and it was for this its writer was happy to leave behind him all he knew before, and the safety of that, when he began the new story.

I feel that our ever-changing outside world and some learnable lessons about writing fiction are always waiting side by side for us to put into connection, if we can. A writer should say this only of himself and offer an example. In a story I wrote recently called "No Place for You, My Love," the outside world—a definite place in it, of course—not only suggested how to write it but repudiated a way I had already tried. What follows has no claim to be critical analysis; it can be called a piece of hindsight from a working point of view.

What changed my story was a trip. I was invited to drive with an acquaintance, one summer day, down south of New Orleans to see that country for the first (and so far, only) time; and when I got back home, full of the landscape I'd seen, I realized that without being aware of it at the time, I had treated the story to my ride, and it had come into my head in an altogether new form. I set to work and wrote the new version from scratch.

As first written, the story told, in subjective terms, of a girl in a claustrophobic predicament: she was caught fast in the over-familiar, monotonous life of her small town, and immobilized further by a prolonged and hopeless love affair; she could see no way out. As a result of my ride, I extricated—not the girl, but the story.

This character had been well sealed inside her world, by nature and circumstance, just where I'd put her. But she was sealed in to the detriment of the story, because I'd made hers the point of view. The primary step now was getting outside her mind; on that instant I made her a girl from the Middle West. (She'd been before what I knew best, a Southerner.) I kept outside her by taking glimpses of her through the eyes of a total stranger: casting off the half-dozen familiars the first girl had around her, I invented a single new character, a man whom I brought into the story *to be* a stranger, and I was to keep out of his mind, too. I had double-locked the doors behind me.

It would have been for nothing had the original impulse behind the story not proved itself alive; it now took on new energy. That country—that once-submerged, strange land of "south from South"—which had so stamped itself upon my imagination put in an unmistakable claim now as the very image of the story's predicament. It pointed out to me at the same time where the real point of view belonged. Once I'd escaped those characters' minds, I saw it was outside them—suspended, hung in the air between two people, fished alive from the surrounding scene. As I wrote further into the story, something more real, more essential, than the characters were on their own was revealing itself. In effect, though the characters numbered only two, there had come to be a sort of third character along on the ride—the presence of a relationship between the two. It was what grew up between them meeting as strangers, went on the excursion with them, nodded back and forth from one to the other—listening, watching, persuading or denying them, enlarging or diminishing them, forgetful sometimes of who they were or what they were doing here—in its domain—and helping or betraying them along.

(Here I think it perhaps should be remembered that characters in a short story have not the size and importance and capacity for development they have in a novel, but are subservient altogether to the story as a whole.)

This third character's role was that of hypnosis—it was what a relationship *can do,* be it however brief, tentative, potential, happy or sinister, ordinary or extraordinary. I wanted to suggest that its being took shape as the strange, compulsive journey itself, was palpable as its climate and mood, the heat of the day—but was its spirit too, a spirit that held territory, that which is seen fleeting past by two vulnerable people who might seize hands on the run. There are moments in the story when I say neither "she felt" nor "he felt" but "they felt."

This is to grant that I rode out of the old story on the back of the girl and then threw away the girl; but I saved my story, for, entirely different as the second version was, it was what I wanted to tell. Now my subject was out in the open, provided at the same time with a place to happen and a way to say it was happening. All I had to do was recognize it, which I did a little late.

Anyone who has visited the actual scene of this story will possibly recognize it when he meets it here, for the story is visual and the place is out of the ordinary. The connection between a story and its setting may not always be so plain. For no matter whether the "likeness" is there for all to see or not, the place, once entered into the writer's mind in a story, is, in the course of writing the story, *functional*.

Thus I wanted to make seen and believed what was to me, in my story's grip, literally apparent—that secret and shadow are taken away in this country by the merciless light that prevails there, by the river that is like an exposed vein of ore, the road that descends as one with the heat— its nerve (these are all terms in the story), and that the heat is also a visual illusion, shimmering and dancing over the waste that stretches ahead. I was writing of a real place, but doing so in order to write about my subject. I was writing of exposure, and the shock of the world; in the end I tried to make the story's inside outside and then leave the shell behind.

The vain courting of imperviousness in the face of exposure is this little story's plot. Deliver us all from the naked in heart, the girl thinks (this is what I kept of her). "So strangeness gently steels us," I read today in a poem of Richard Wilbur's. Riding down together into strange country is danger, a play at danger, secretly poetic, and the characters, in attempting it as a mutual feat, admit nothing to each other except the wicked heat and its comical inconvenience. The only time they will yield or touch is while they are dancing in the crowd that to them is comically unlikely (hence insulating, nonconducting) or taking a kiss outside time. Nevertheless it happens that they go along aware, from moment to moment, as one: as my third character, the straining, hallucinatory eyes and ears, the roused-up sentient being of that place. Exposure begins in intuition; and the intuition comes to its end in showing the heart that has expected, while it dreads, that exposure.

Writing it as I'd done before, as a story of concealment, in terms of the hermetic and the familiar, had somehow resulted in my own effective concealment of what I meant to show.

Now, the place had suggested to me that something demoniac was called for—the speed of the ride pitted against the danger of an easy or conventionally tempting sympathy, the heat that in itself drives on the driver in the face of an inimical world. Something wilder than ordinary communication between well-disposed strangers, and more ruthless and more tender, more pressing and acute, than their automatic, saving ironies and graces, I felt, and do so often feel, has to come up against a world like that.

I did my best to merge, or even to identify, the abstract with the concrete as it became possible in this story—where setting, characters, mood, and method of writing all worked as parts of the same thing and subject to related laws and conditionings. The story *had* to be self-evident, and to hold its speed to the end—a speed I think of as racing, though it may not seem so to the reader.

Above all, I had no wish to sound mystical, but I admit that I did expect to sound mysterious now and then, if I could: this was a circumstantial, realistic story in which the reality *was* mystery. The cry that rose up at the story's end was, I hope unmistakably, the cry of that doomed relationship—personal, mortal, psychic—admitted in order to be denied, a cry that the characters were first able (and prone) to listen to, and then able in part to ignore. The cry was authentic to my story: the end of a journey *can* set up a cry, the shallowest provocation to sympathy and love does hate to give up the ghost. A relationship of the most fleeting kind has the power inherent to loom like a

genie—to become vocative at the last, as it has already become present and taken up room; as it has spread out as a
destination however unlikely; as it has glimmered and
rushed by in the dark and dust outside, showing occasional
points of fire. Relationship *is* a pervading and changing
mystery; it is not words that make it so in life, but words
have to make it so in a story. Brutal or lovely, the mystery
waits for people wherever they go, whatever extreme they
run to.

I had got back at the end of the new story to suggesting
what I had taken as the point of departure in the old, but
there was no question in my mind which story was nearer
the mark of my intention. This may not reflect very well
on the brightness of the author at work; it may cause a
reader to wonder how often a story has to rescue itself. I
think it goes to show, all the same, that subject, method,
form, style, all wait upon—indeed hang upon—a sort of
double thunderclap at the author's ears: the break of the
living world upon what is already stirring inside the mind,
and the answering impulse that in a moment of high consciousness fuses impact and image and fires them off together. There never really was a sound, but the impact is
always recognizable, granting the author's sensitivity and
sense; and if the impulse so projected is to some degree
fulfilled, it may give some pleasure in its course to the
writer and reader. The living world itself remains just the
same as it always was, and luckily enough for the story,
among other things, for it can test and talk back to the story
any day in the week. Between the writer and the story he
writes, *there* is the undying third character.

PLACE IN FICTION

Place is one of the lesser angels that watch over the racing hand of fiction, perhaps the one that gazes benignly enough from off to one side, while others, like character, plot, symbolic meaning, and so on, are doing a good deal of wing-beating about her chair, and feeling, who in my eyes carries the crown, soars highest of them all and rightly relegates place into the shade. Nevertheless, it is this lowlier angel that concerns us here. There have been signs that she has been rather neglected of late; maybe she could do with a little petitioning.

What place has place in fiction? It might be thought so modest a one that it can be taken for granted: the location of a novel; to use a term of the day, it may make the novel "regional." The term, like most terms used to pin down a novel, means little; and Henry James said there isn't any difference between "the English novel" and "the American novel," since there are only two kinds of novels at all, the good and the bad. Of course Henry James didn't stop there, and we all hate generalities, and so does place. Yet as soon as we step down from the general view to the close and particular, as writers must and readers may and teachers well know how to, and consider what good writing may be, place can be seen, in her own way, to have a great deal to do with that goodness, if not to be responsible for it. How so?

First, with the goodness—validity—in the raw material of writing. Second, with the goodness in the writing itself—the achieved world of appearance, through which the novelist has his whole say and puts his whole case. There will still be the lady, always, who dismissed *The Ancient Mariner* on grounds of implausibility. Third, with the goodness—the worth—in the writer himself: place is where he has his roots, place is where he stands; in his experience out of which he writes, it provides the base of reference; in his work, the point of view. Let us consider place in fiction in these three wide aspects.

Wide, but of course connected—vitally so. And if in some present-day novels the connection has apparently slipped, that makes a fresh reason for us to ponder the subject of place. For novels, besides being the pleasantest things imaginable, are powerful forces on the side. Mutual understanding in the world being nearly always, as now, at low ebb, it is comforting to remember that it is through art that one country can nearly always speak reliably to another, if the other can hear at all. Art, though, is never the voice of a country; it is an even more precious thing, the voice of the individual, doing its best to speak, not comfort of any sort, indeed, but truth. And the art that speaks it most unmistakably, most directly, most variously, most fully, is fiction; in particular, the novel.

Why? Because the novel from the start has been bound up in the local, the "real," the present, the ordinary day-to-day of human experience. Where the imagination comes in is in directing the use of all this. That use is endless, and there are only four words, of all the millions we've hatched, that a novel rules out: "Once upon a time." They make a story a fairy tale by the simple sweep of the remove—by abolishing the present and the place where we are instead of conveying them to us. Of course we shall have some sort of fairy tale with us always—just now it is the historical novel. Fiction is properly at work on the here and now, or the past made here and now; for in novels *we* have to be there. Fiction provides the ideal texture through which the feeling and meaning that permeate our own personal, present lives will best show through. For in his theme—the most vital and important part of the work at hand—the novelist has the blessing of the inexhaustible subject: you and me. You and me, here. Inside that generous scope and circumference—who could ask for anything more?—the novel can accommodate practically anything on earth; and has abundantly done so. The novel so long as it be *alive* gives pleasure, and must always give pleasure, enough to stave off the departure of the Wedding Guest forever, except for that one lady.

It is by the nature of itself that fiction is all bound up in the local. The internal reason for that is surely that *feelings* are bound up in place. The human mind is a mass of associations—associations more poetic even than actual. I say, "The Yorkshire Moors," and you will say, *"Wuthering Heights,"* and I have only to murmur, "If Father were only alive—" for you to come back with "We could go to Moscow," which certainly is not even so. The truth is, fiction depends for its life on place. Location is the crossroads of circumstance, the proving ground of "What happened? Who's here? Who's coming?"—and that is the heart's field.

Unpredictable as the future of any art must be, one condition we may hazard about writing: of all the arts, it is the one least likely to cut the cord that binds it to its source. Music and dancing, while originating out of place—groves!—and perhaps invoking it still to minds pure or childlike, are no longer bound to dwell there. Sculpture exists out in empty space: that is what it commands and replies to. Toward painting, place, to be so highly visible, has had a curious and changing relationship. Indeed, wasn't it when landscape invaded painting, and painting was given, with the profane content, a narrative content, that this worked to bring on a revolution to the art? Impressionism brought not the likeness-to-life but the mystery of place onto canvas; it was the method, not the subject, that told this. Painting and writing, always the closest two of the sister arts (and in ancient Chinese days only the blink of an eye seems to have separated them), have each a still closer connection with place than they have with each other; but a difference lies in their respective requirements of it, and even further in the way they use it—the written word being ultimately as different from the pigment as the note of the scale is from the chisel.

One element, which has just been mentioned, is surely the underlying bond that connects all the arts with place. All of them celebrate its mystery. Where does this mystery lie? Is it in the fact that place has a more lasting identity than we have, and we unswervingly tend to attach ourselves to identity? Might the magic lie partly, too, in the *name* of the place—since that is what *we* gave it? Surely, once we have it named, we have put a kind of poetic claim on its existence; the claim works even out of sight—may work forever sight unseen. The Seven Wonders of the World still give us this poetic kind of gratification. And notice we do not say simply "The Hanging Gardens"—that would leave them dangling out of reach and dubious in nature; we say "The Hanging Gardens of Babylon," and there they are, before our eyes, shimmering and garlanded and exactly elevated to the Babylonian measurement.

Edward Lear tapped his unerring finger on the magic of place in the limerick. There's something unutterably convincing about that Old Person of Sparta who had twenty-five sons and one darta, and it is surely beyond question that he fed them on snails and weighed them in scales, because we know where that Old Person is *from*—Sparta! We certainly do not need further to be told his *name*. "Consider the source." Experience has ever advised us to base validity on point of origin.

Being shown how to locate, to place, any account is what does most toward *making* us believe it, not merely allowing us to, may the account be the facts or a lie; and that is where place in fiction comes in. Fiction is a lie. Never in its inside thoughts, always in its outside dress.

Some of us grew up with the china night-light, the little lamp whose lighting showed its secret and with that spread enchantment. The outside is painted with a scene, which is one thing; then, when the lamp is lighted, through the porcelain sides a new picture comes out through the old, and they are seen as one. A lamp I knew of was a view of London till it was lit; but then it was the Great Fire of London, and you could go beautifully to sleep by it. The lamp alight is the combination of internal and external, glowing at the imagination as one; and so is the good novel. Seeing that these inner and outer surfaces do lie so close together and so implicit in each other, the wonder is that human life so often separates them, or appears to, and it takes a good novel to put them back together.

The good novel should be steadily alight, revealing. Before it can hope to be that, it must of course be steadily visible from its outside, presenting a continuous, shapely, pleasing and finished surface to the eye.

The sense of a story when the visibility is only partial or intermittent is as endangered as Eliza crossing the ice. Forty hounds of confusion are after it, the black waters of disbelief open up between its steps, and no matter which way it jumps it is bound to slip. Even if it has a little baby moral in its arms, it is more than likely a goner.

The novel must get Eliza across the ice; what it means—the way it proceeds—is always in jeopardy. It must be given a surface that is continuous and unbroken, never too thin to trust, always in touch with the senses. Its world of experience must be at every step, through every moment, within reach as the world of appearance.

This makes it the business of writing, and the responsibility of the writer, to disentangle the significant—in character, incident, setting, mood, everything—from the random and meaningless and irrelevant that in real life surround and beset it. It is a matter of his selecting and, by all that implies, of changing "real" life as he goes. With each word he writes, he acts—as literally and methodically as if he hacked his way through a forest and blazed it for the word that follows. He makes choices at the explicit demand of this one present story; each choice implies, explains, limits the next, and illuminates the one before. No two stories ever go the same way, although in different hands one story might possibly go any one of a thousand ways; and though the woods may look the same from outside, it is a new and different labyrinth every time. What tells the author his way? Nothing at all but what he knows inside himself: the same thing that hints to him afterward how far he has missed it, how near he may have come to the heart of it. In a working sense, the novel and its place have become one: work has made them, for the time being, the same thing, like the explorer's tentative map of the known world.

The reason why every word you write in a good novel is a lie, then, is that it is written expressly to serve the purpose; if it does not apply, it is fancy and frivolous, however specially dear to the writer's heart. Actuality, it is true, is an even bigger risk to the novel than fancy writing is, being frequently even more confusing, irrelevant, diluted and generally far-fetched than ill-chosen words can make it. Yet somehow, the world of appearance in the novel has got to *seem* actuality. Is there a reliable solution to the problem? Place being brought to life in the round before the reader's eye is the readiest and gentlest and most honest and natural way this can be brought about, I think; every instinct advises it. The moment the place in which the novel happens is accepted as true, through it will begin to glow, in a kind of recognizable glory, the feeling and thought that inhabited the novel in the author's head and animated the whole of his work.

Besides furnishing a plausible abode for the novel's world of feeling, place has a good deal to do with making the characters real, that is, themselves, and keeping them so. The reason is simply that, as Tristram Shandy observed,

"We are not made of glass, as characters on Mercury might be." Place *can* be transparent, or translucent: not people. In real life we have to express the things plainest and closest to our minds by the clumsy word and the half-finished gesture; the chances are our most usual behavior makes sense only in a kind of daily way, because it has become familiar to our nearest and dearest, and still demands their constant indulgence and understanding. It is our describable outside that defines us, willy-nilly, to others, that may save us, or destroy us, in the world; it may be our shield against chaos, our mask against exposure; but whatever it is, the move we make in the place we live has to signify our intent and meaning.

Then think how unprotected the poor character in a novel is, into whose mind the author is inviting us to look—unprotected and hence surely unbelievable! But no, the author has expressly seen to believability. Though he must know all, again he works with illusion. Just as the world of a novel is more highly selective than that of real life, so character in a novel is much more definite, less shadowy than our own, in order that we may believe in it. This is not to say that the character's scope must be limited; it is our vision of it that is guided. It is a kind of phenomenon of writing that the likeliest character has first to be enclosed inside the bounds of even greater likelihood, or he will fly to pieces. Paradoxically, the more narrowly we can examine a fictional character, the greater he is likely to loom up. We must see him set to scale in his proper world to know his size. Place, then, has the most delicate control over character too: by confining character, it defines it.

Place in fiction is the named, identified, concrete, exact

and exacting, and therefore credible, gathering spot of all
that has been felt, is about to be experienced, in the novel's
progress. Location pertains to feeling; feeling profoundly
pertains to place; place in history partakes of feeling, as
feeling about history partakes of place. Every story would
be another story, and unrecognizable as art, if it took up its
characters and plot and happened somewhere else. Imag-
ine *Swann's Way* laid in London, or *The Magic Mountain* in
Spain, or *Green Mansions* in the Black Forest. The very notion of moving a novel brings ruder havoc to the mind and
affections than would a century's alteration in its time. It is
only too easy to conceive that a bomb that could destroy all
trace of places as we know them, in life and through books,
could also destroy all feelings as we know them, so irre-
trievably and so happily are recognition, memory, history,
valor, love, all the instincts of poetry and praise, worship
and endeavor, bound up in place. From the dawn of man's
imagination, place has enshrined the spirit; as soon as man
stopped wandering and stood still and looked about him,
he found a god in that place; and from then on, that was
where the god abided and spoke from if ever he spoke.

Feelings are bound up in place, and in art, from time to
time, place undoubtedly works upon genius. Can anyone
well explain otherwise what makes a given dot on the map
come passionately alive, for good and all, in a novel—like
one of those novae that suddenly blaze with inexplicable
fire in the heavens? What brought a *Wuthering Heights* out of
Yorkshire, or a *Sound and the Fury* out of Mississippi?

If place does work upon genius, how does it? It may be
that place can focus the gigantic, voracious eye of genius
and bring its gaze to point. Focus then means awareness,
discernment, order, clarity, insight—they are like the at-

tributes of love. The act of focusing itself has beauty and meaning; it is the act that, continued in, turns into mediation, into poetry. Indeed, as soon as the least of us stands still, that is the moment something extraordinary is seen to be going on in the world. The drama, old beyond count as it is, is no older than the first stage. Without the amphitheatre around it to persuade the ear and bend the eye upon a point, how could poetry ever have been spoken, how have been heard? Man is articulate and intelligible only when he begins to communicate inside the strict terms of poetry and reason. Symbols in the end, both are permanent forms of the act of focusing.

Surely place induces poetry, and when the poet is extremely attentive to what is there, a meaning may even attach to his poem out of the spot on earth where it is spoken, and the poem signify the more because it does spring so wholly out of its place, and the sap has run up into it as into a tree.

But we had better confine ourselves here to prose. And then, to take the most absolutely unfanciful novelist of them all, it is to hear him saying, *"Madame Bovary—c'est moi."* And we see focusing become so intent and aware and conscious in this most "realistic" novel of them all as to amount to fusion. Flaubert's work is indeed of the kind that is embedded immovably as rock in the country of its birth. If, with the slicers of any old (or new) criticism at all, you were to cut down through *Madame Bovary*, its cross section would still be the same as the cross section of that living earth, in texture, color, composition, all; which would be no surprise to Flaubert. For such fusion always means accomplishment no less conscious than it is gigantic—effort that must exist entirely as its own reward. We all know the letter Flaubert wrote when he had just found, in the morning paper, in an account of a minister's visit to Rouen, a phrase in the Mayor's speech of welcome

> which I had written the day before, textually, in my *Bovary*... Not only were the idea and the words the same, but even the rhythm of the style. It's things like this that give me pleasure... Everything one invents is true, you may be perfectly sure of that! Poetry is as precise as geometry... And besides, after reaching a certain point, one no longer makes any mistakes about the things of the soul. My poor Bovary, without a doubt, is suffering and weeping this very instant in twenty villages of France.

And now that we have come to the writer himself, the question of place resolves itself into the point of view. In this changeover from the objective to the subjective, wonderful and unexpected variations may occur.

Place, to the writer at work, is seen in a frame. Not an empty frame, a brimming one. Point of view is a sort of burning-glass, a product of personal experience and time; it is burnished with feelings and sensibilities, charged from moment to moment with the sun-points of imagination. It is an instrument—one of intensification; it acts, it behaves, it is temperamental. We have seen that the writer must accurately choose, combine, superimpose upon, blot out, shake up, alter the outside world for one absolute purpose, the good of his story. To do this, he is always seeing double, two pictures at once in his frame, his and the world's, a fact that he constantly comprehends; and he works best in a state of constant and subtle and unfooled reference between the two. It is his clear intention—his passion, I should say—to make the reader see only one of the pictures—the author's—under the pleasing illusion that it is the world's; this enormity is the accomplishment of a good story. I think it likely that at the moment of the writer's highest awareness of, and responsiveness to, the "real" world, his imagination's choice (and miles away it may be from actuality) comes closest to being infallible for his purpose. For the spirit of things is what is sought. No blur of inexactness, no cloud of vagueness, is allowable in good writing; from the first seeing to the last putting down, there must be steady lucidity and uncompromise of purpose. I speak, of course, of the ideal.

One of the most important things the young writer comes to see for himself is that point of view *is* an instrument, not an end in itself, that is useful as a glass, and not as a mirror to reflect a dear and pensive face. Conscientiously used, point of view will discover, explore, see through—it may sometimes divine and prophesy. Misused, it turns opaque almost at once and gets in the way of the book. And when the good novel is finished, its cooled outside shape, what Sean O'Faolain has called "the veil of reality," has all the burden of communicating that initial, spontaneous, overwhelming, driving charge of personal inner feeling that was the novel's reason for being. The measure of this representation of life corresponds most tellingly with the novel's life expectancy: whenever its world of outside appearance grows dim or false to the eye, the novel has expired.

Establishing a chink-proof world of appearance is not only the first responsibility of the writer; it is the primary step in the technique of every sort of fiction: lyric and romantic, of course; the "realistic," it goes without saying; and other sorts as well. Fantasy itself must touch ground with at least one toe, and ghost stories must have one foot, so to speak, in the grave. The black, squat, hairy ghosts of M. R. James come right out of Cambridge. Only fantasy's stepchild, poor science-fiction, does not touch earth anywhere; and it is doubtful already if happenings entirely confined to outer space are ever going to move us, or even divert us for long. Satire, engaged in its most intellectual of exercises, must first of all establish an impeccable *locus operandi;* its premise is the kingdom where certain rules apply. The countries Gulliver visits are the systems of thought and learning Swift satirizes made visible one after the other and set in operation. But while place in satire is a purely artificial construction, set up to be knocked down, in humor place becomes its most revealing and at the same time is itself the most revealed. This is because humor, it seems to me, of all forms of fiction, entirely accepts place for what it is.

"Spotted Horses," by William Faulkner, is a good case in point. At the same time that this is just about Mr. Faulkner's funniest story, it is the most thorough and faithful picture of a Mississippi crossroads hamlet that you could ever hope to see. True in spirit, it is also true to everyday fact. Faulkner's art, which often lets him shoot the moon, tells him when to be literal too. In all its specification of detail, both mundane and poetic, in its complete adherence to social fact (which nobody knows better than Faulkner, surely, in writing today), by its unerring aim of observation as true as the sights of a gun would give, but Faulkner has no malice, only compassion; and even and also in the joy of those elements of harlequinade-fantasy that the spotted horses of the title bring in—in all that shining fidelity to place lies the heart and secret of this tale's comic glory.

Faulkner is, of course, the triumphant example in America today of the mastery of place in fiction. Yoknapatawpha County, so supremely and exclusively and majestically and totally itself, is an everywhere, but only because Faulkner's first concern is for what comes first—Yoknapatawpha, his own created world. I am not sure, as a Mississippian myself, how widely it is realized and appreciated that these works of such marvelous imaginative power can also stand as works of the carefulest and purest representation. Heightened, of course: their specialty is they are twice as true as life, and that is why it takes a genius to write them. "Spotted Horses" may not have happened yet; if it had, some others might have tried to make a story of it; but "Spotted Horses" could happen tomorrow—that is one of its glories. It could happen today or tomorrow at any little crossroads hamlet in Mississippi; the whole combination of irresistibility is there. We have the Snopses ready, the Mrs. Littlejohns ready, nice Ratliff and the Judge ready and sighing, the clowns, sober and merry, settled for the evening retrospection of it in the cool dusk of the porch; and the Henry Armstids armed with their obsessions, the little periwinkle-eyed boys armed with their indestructibility; the beautiful, overweening spring, too, the moonlight on the pear trees from which the mockingbird's song keeps returning; and the little store and the fat boy to steal and steal away at its candy. There are undoubtedly spotted horses too, in the offing—somewhere in Texas this minute, straining toward the day. After Faulkner has told it, it is easy for one and all to look back and see it.

Faulkner, simply, knew it already; it is a different kind of knowledge from Flaubert's, and proof could not add much to it. He was born knowing, or rather learning, or rather prophesying, all that and more; and having it all together at one time available while he writes is one of the marks of his mind. If there *is* any more in Mississippi than is engaged and dilated upon, and made twice as real as it used to be and applies now to the world, in the one story "Spotted Horses," then we would almost rather not know it— but I don't bet a piece of store candy that there is. In Faulkner's humor, even more measurably than in his tragedy, it is all there.

It may be going too far to say that the exactness and concreteness and solidity of the real world achieved in a story correspond to the intensity of feeling in the author's mind and to the very turn of his heart; but there lies the secret of our confidence in him.

Making reality real is art's responsibility. It is a practical assignment, then, a self-assignment: to achieve, by a cultivated sensitivity for observing life, a capacity for receiving its impressions, a lonely, unremitting, unaided, unaidable vision, and transferring this vision without distortion to it onto the pages of a novel, where, if the reader is so persuaded, it will turn into the reader's illusion. How bent on this peculiar joy we are, reader and writer, willingly to practice, willingly to undergo, this alchemy for it!

What is there, then, about place that is transferable to the pages of a novel? The best things—the explicit things: physical texture. And as place has functioned between the writer and his material, so it functions between the writer and reader. Location is the ground conductor of all the currents of emotion and belief and moral conviction that charge out from the story in its course. These charges need the warm hard earth underfoot, the light and lift of air, the stir and play of mood, the softening bath of atmosphere that give the likeness-to-life that life needs. Through the story's translation and ordering of life, the unconvincing raw material becomes the very heart's familiar. Life *is* strange. Stories hardly make it more so; with all they are able to tell and surmise, they make it more believably, more inevitably so.

I think the sense of place is as essential to good and honest writing as a logical mind; surely they are somewhere related. It is by knowing where you stand that you grow able to judge where you are. Place absorbs our earliest notice and attention, it bestows on us our original awareness; and our critical powers spring up from the study of it and the growth of experience inside it. It perseveres in bringing us back to earth when we fly too high. It never really stops informing us, for it is forever astir, alive, changing, reflecting, like the mind of man itself. One place comprehended can make us understand other places better. Sense of place gives equilibrium; extended, it is sense of direction too. Carried off we might be in spirit, and should be, when we are reading or writing something good; but it is the sense of place going with us still that is the ball of golden thread to carry us there and back and in every sense of the word to bring us home.

What can place *not* give? Theme. It can present theme, show it to the last detail—but place is forever illustrative: it is a picture of what man has done and imagined, it is his visible past, result. Human life is fiction's only theme.

—

Should the writer, then, write about home? It is both natural and sensible that the place where we have our roots
should become the setting, the first and primary proving
ground, of our fiction. Location, however, is not simply to
be used by the writer—it is to be discovered, as each novel
itself, in the act of writing, is discovery. Discovery does not
imply that the place is new, only that we are. Place is as old
as the hills. Kilroy at least has been there, and left his name.
Discovery, not being a matter of writing our name on a
wall, but of seeing what that wall is, and what is over it, is a
matter of vision.

One can no more say, "To write stay home," than one
can say, "To write leave home." It is the writing that makes
its own rules and conditions for each person. And though
place is home, it is for the writer writing simply *locus*. It is
where the particular story he writes can be pinned down,
the circle it can spin through and keep the state of grace, so
that for the story's duration the rest of the world suspends
its claim upon it and lies low as the story in peaceful extension, the *locus* fading off into the blue.

Naturally, it is the very breath of life, whether one
writes a word of fiction or not, to go out and see what is to
be seen of the world. For the artist to be unwilling to move,
mentally or spiritually or physically, out of the familiar is a
sign that spiritual timidity or poverty or decay has come
upon him; for what is familiar will then have turned into all
that is tyrannical.

One can only say: writers must always write best of what
they know, and sometimes they do it by staying where they
know it. But not for safety's sake. Although it is in the
words of a witch—or all the more because of that—a

comment of Hecate's in *Macbeth* is worth our heed: "Security/ Is mortal's chiefest enemy." In fact, when we think in terms of the spirit, which are the terms of writing, is there a conception more stupefying than that of security? Yet writing of what you know has nothing to do with security: what is more dangerous? How can you go out on a limb if you do not know your own tree? No art ever came out of not risking your neck. And risk—experiment—is a considerable part of the joy of doing, which is the lone, simple reason all writers of serious fiction are willing to work as hard as they do.

The open mind and the receptive heart—which are at last and with fortune's smile the informed mind and the experienced heart—are to be gained anywhere, any time, without necessarily moving an inch from any present address. There must surely be as many ways of seeing a place as there are pairs of eyes to see it. The impact happens in so many different ways.

It may be the stranger within the gates whose eye is smitten by the crucial thing, the essence of life, the moment or act in our long-familiar midst that will forever define it. The inhabitant who has taken his fill of a place and gone away may look back and see it for good, from afar, still there in his mind's eye like a city over the hill. It was in the New Zealand stories, written eleven thousand miles from home and out of homesickness, that Katherine Mansfield came into her own. Joyce transplanted not his subject but himself while writing about it, and it was as though he had never left it at all: there it was, still in his eye, exactly the way he had last seen it. From the Continent he wrote the life of Dublin as it was then into a book of the future, for he went translating his own language of it on and on into a country of its own, where it set up a kingdom as renowned as Prester John's. Sometimes two places, two countries, are brought to bear on each other, as in E. M. Forster's work, and the heart of the novel is heard beating most plainly, most passionately, most personally when two places are at meeting point.

There may come to be new places in our lives that are second spiritual homes—closer to us in some ways, perhaps, than our original homes. But the home tie is the blood tie. And had it meant nothing to us, any other place thereafter would have meant less, and we would carry no compass inside ourselves to find home ever, anywhere at all. We would not even guess what we had missed.

It is noticeable that those writers who for their own good reasons push out against their backgrounds nearly always passionately adopt the new one in their work. Revolt itself is a reference and tribute to the potency of what is left behind. The substitute place, the adopted country, is sometimes a very much stricter, bolder, or harsher one than the original, seldom more lax or undemanding—showing that what was wanted was structure, definition, rigidity—perhaps these were wanted, and understanding was not.

Hemingway in our time has sought out the formal and ruthless territories of the world, archaic ones often, where there are bullfight arenas, theatres of hunting and war, places with a primitive, or formidable, stripped-down character, with implacable codes, with inscrutable justices and inevitable retributions. But whatever the scene of his work, it is the *places* that never are hostile. People give pain, are callous and insensitive, empty and cruel, carrying with them no pasts as they promise no futures. But place heals the hurt, soothes the outrage, fills the terrible vacuum that these human beings make. It heals actively, and the response is given consciously, with the ardent care and explicitness, respect and delight of a lover, when fishing streams or naming over streets becomes almost something of the lover's secret language—as the careful conversations between characters in Hemingway bear hints of the secret language of hate. The response to place has the added intensity that comes with the place's not being native or taken for granted, but found, chosen; thereby is the rest more heavily repudiated. It is the response of the aficionado; the response, too, is adopted. The title "A Clean Well Lighted Place" is just what the human being is not, for Hemingway, and perhaps it is the epitome of what man would like to find in his fellowman but never has yet, says the author, and never is going to.

We see that point of view is hardly a single, unalterable vision, but a profound and developing one of great complexity. The vision itself may move in and out of its material, shuttle-fashion, instead of being simply turned on it, like a telescope on the moon. Writing is an expression of the writer's own peculiar personality, could not help being so. Yet in reading great works one feels that the finished piece transcends the personal. All writers great and small must sometimes have felt that they have become part of what they wrote even more than it still remains a part of them.

When I speak of writing from where you have put down roots, it may be said that what I urge is "regional" writing. "Regional," I think, is a careless term, as well as a condescending one, because what it does is fail to differentiate between the localized raw material of life and its outcome as art. "Regional" is an outsider's term; it has no meaning for the insider who is doing the writing, because as far as he knows he is simply writing about life. Jane Austen, Emily Brontë, Thomas Hardy, Cervantes, Turgenev, the authors of the books of the Old Testament, all confined themselves to regions, great or small—but are they regional? Then who from the start of time has not been so?

It may well be said that all work springing out of such vital impulse from its native soil has certain things in common. But what signifies is that these are not the little things that it takes a fine-tooth critic to search out, but the great things, that could not be missed or mistaken, for they are the beacon lights of literature.

It seems plain that the art that speaks most clearly, explicitly, directly and passionately from its place of origin will remain the longest understood. It is through place that we put out roots, wherever birth, chance, fate or our traveling selves set us down; but where those roots reach toward—whether in America, England or Timbuktu—is the deep and running vein, eternal and consistent and everywhere purely itself, that feeds and is fed by the human understanding. The challenge to writers today, I think, is not to disown any part of our heritage. Whatever our theme in writing, it is old and tried. Whatever our place, it has been visited by the stranger, it will never be new again. It is only the vision that can be new; but that is enough.

1956

WORDS INTO FICTION

We start from scratch, and words don't; which is the thing that matters—matters over and over again. For though we grow up in the language, when we begin using words to make a piece of fiction, that is of course as different from using even the same words to say hello on the telephone as putting paint on canvas is. This very leap in the dark is exactly what writers write fiction in order to try. And surely they discovered that daring, and developed that wish, from reading. My feeling is that it's when reading begins to impress on us what degrees and degrees and degrees of communication are possible between novelists and ourselves as readers that we surmise what it has meant, can mean, to write novels.

Indeed, learning to write may be a part of learning to read. For all I know, writing comes out of a superior devotion to reading. I feel sure that serious writing does come, must come, out of devotion to the thing itself, to fiction as an art. Both reading and writing are experiences—lifelong—

in the course of which we who encounter words used in certain ways are persuaded by them to be brought mind and heart within the presence, the power, of the imagination. This we find to be above all the power to reveal, with nothing barred.

But of course writing fiction, which comes out of life and has the object of showing it, can't be learned from copying out of books. Imitation, or what is in any respect secondhand, is precisely what writing is not. How it is learned can only remain in general—like all else that is personal—an open question; and if ever it's called settled, or solved, the day of fiction is already over. The solution will be the last rites at the funeral. Only the writing of fiction keeps fiction alive. Regardless of whether or not it is reading that gives writing birth, a society that no longer writes novels is not very likely to read any novels at all.

Since we must and do write each our own way, we may during actual writing get more lasting instruction not from another's work, whatever its blessings, however better it is than ours, but from our own poor scratched-over pages. For these we can hold up to life. That is, we are born with a mind and heart to hold each page up to, and to ask: is it valid?

Reading the work of other writers and in the whole, and our long thoughts in retrospect, can tell us all we are able to know of fiction and at firsthand, but this is about *reading*.

The writer himself studies intensely how to do it while he is in the thick of doing it; then when the particular novel or story is done, he is likely to forget how; he does well to. Each work is new. Mercifully, the question of *how* abides less in the abstract, and less in the past, than in the specific, in the work at hand; I chance saying this is so with most writers. Maybe some particular problems, with their confusions and might-have-beens, could be seen into with profit just at the windup, but more likely it's already too late. Already the *working* insight, which is what counts, is gone—along with the story it made, that made it.

And rightly. Fiction finished has to bear the responsibility of its own meaning, it is its own memory. It is now a thing apart from the writer; like a letter mailed, it is nearer by now to its reader. If the writer has had luck, it has something of its own to travel on, something that can make it persist for a while, an identity, before it must fade.

How can I express outside fiction what I think this reality of fiction is?

As a child I was led, an unwilling sightseer, into Mammoth Cave in Kentucky, and after our party had been halted in the blackest hole yet and our guide had let us wait guessing in cold dark what would happen to us, suddenly a light was struck. And we stood in a prism. The chamber was bathed in color, and there was nothing else, we and our guide alike were blotted out by radiance. As I remember, nobody said boo. Gradually we could make out that there was a river in the floor, black as night, which appeared to come out of a closet in the wall; and then, on it, a common rowboat, with ordinary countrified people like ourselves sitting in it, mute, wearing hats, came floating out and on by, and exited into the closet in the opposite wall. I suppose they were simply a party taking the more expensive tour. As we tourists mutually and silently stared, our guide treated us to a recitation on bats, how they lived in uncounted numbers down here and reached light by shooting up winding mile-high chimneys through rock, never touching by so much as the crook of a wing. He had memorized the speech, and we didn't see a bat. Then the light was put out—just as it is after you've had your two cents' worth in the Baptistry of Florence, where of course more happens: the thing I'm trying here to leave out. As again we stood damp and cold and not able to see our feet, while we each now had something of our own out of it, presumably, what I for one remember is how right I had been in telling my parents it would be a bore. For I was too ignorant to know there might be more, or even less, in there than I could see unaided.

Fiction is not the cave; and human life, fiction's territory, merely contains caves. I am only trying to express what I think the so-called raw material is *without its interpretation;* without its artist. Without the act of human understanding—and it is a double act through which we make sense to each other—experience is the worst kind of emptiness; it is obliteration, black or prismatic, as meaningless as was indeed that loveless cave. Before there is meaning, there has to occur some personal act of vision. And it is this that is continuously projected as the novelist writes, and again as we, each to ourselves, read.

If this makes fiction sound full of mystery, I think it's fuller than I know how to say. Plot, characters, setting and so forth, are not what I'm referring to now; we all deal with those as best we can. The mystery lies in the use of language to express human life.

In writing, do we try to solve this mystery? No, I think we take hold of the other end of the stick. In very practical ways, we rediscover the mystery. We even, I might say, take advantage of it.

As we know, a body of criticism stands ready to provide its solution, which is a kind of translation of fiction into another language. It offers us close analysis, like a headphone we can clamp on at the U.N. when they are speaking the Arabian tongue. I feel that we can accept this but only with distinct reservations—not about its brilliance or its worth, but about its time and place of application. While we are in the middle of reading some novel, the possibility of the critical phrase "in other words" is one to destroy, rather than make for, a real—that is, imaginative—understanding of the author. Indeed, it is one sure way to break off his carefully laid connection.

Fiction is made to show forth human life, in some chosen part and aspect. A year or so of one writer's life has gone into the writing of a novel, and then to the reader— so long at least as he is reading it—it may be something in his life. There is a remarkable chance of give-and-take. Does this not suggest that, in the novel at least, words have been found for which there may be no other words? If fiction matters—and many lives are at stake that it does— there can be, for the duration of the book, *no* other words.

The point for us if we write is that nearly everything we can learn about writing can be set down only in fiction's terms. What we know about writing the novel *is* the novel.

Try to tear it down, take it back to its beginning, and you are not so much lost as simply nowhere. Some things once done you can't undo, and I hope and believe fiction is one of them. What its own author knows about a novel is flexible till the end; it changes as it goes, and more than that, it will not be the same knowledge he has by the time the work ends as he had when it began. There is a difference not so much in measure of knowledge, which you would take for granted, as in kind of knowledge. The idea is now the object. The idea is something that you or I might just conceivably have had in common with the author, in the vague free air of the everyday. But not by the wildest chance should we be able to duplicate by one sentence what happened to the idea; neither could the author himself write the same novel again. As he works, his own revision, even though he throws away his changes, can never be wholly undone. The novel has passed through that station on its track. And as readers, we too proceed by the author's arbitrary direction to his one-time-only destination: a journey rather strange, hardly in a straight line, altogether personal.

There has occurred the experience of the writer in writing the novel, and now there occurs the experience of the reader in reading it. More than one mind and heart go into this. We may even hope to follow into a kind of future with a novel that to us seems good, drawn forward by what the long unfolding has promised and so far revealed. By yielding to what has been, by all his available means, *suggested*, we are able to see for ourselves a certain distance beyond what is possible for him simply to *say*. So that, although nobody else ought to say this, the novelist *has* said, "In other words . . ."

Thus all fiction may be seen as a symbol, if this is desired—and how often it is, so it seems. But surely the novel exists within the big symbol of fiction itself—not the other way round, as a conglomeration of little symbols. I think that fiction is the hen, not the egg, and that the good live hen came first.

Certainly symbols fill our daily lives, our busily communicative, if not always communicating, world; and any number of them come with perfect naturalness into our daily conversation and our behavior. And they are a legitimate part of fiction, as they have always been of every art—desirable as any device is, so long as it serves art. Symbols have to spring from the work direct, and stay alive. Symbols for the sake of symbols are counterfeit, and were they all stamped on the page in red they couldn't any more quickly give themselves away. So are symbols failing their purpose when they don't keep to proportion in the book. However alive they are, they should never call for an emphasis greater than the emotional reality they serve, in their moment, to illuminate. One way of looking at Moby Dick is that his task as a symbol was so big and strenuous that he *had* to be a whale.

Most symbols that a fiction writer uses, however carefully, today are apt to be as swiftly spotted by his reader as the smoke signals that once crossed our plains from Indian to Indian. Using symbols and—still worse—finding symbols is such a habit. It follows that too little comes to be suggested, and this, as can never be affirmed often enough, is the purpose of every word that goes into a piece of fiction. The imagination has to be involved, and more—ignited.

How much brighter than the symbol can be the explicit observation that springs firsthand from deep and present feeling in one breast. Indeed, it is something like this, spontaneous in effect, pure in effect, that takes on the emotional value of a symbol when it was first minted, but which as time passes shrinks to become only a counter.

When Chekhov says there were so many stars out that one could not have put a finger between them, he gives us more than night, he gives us *that* night. For symbols can only grow to be the same when the same experiences on which fiction is based are more and more partaken of by us all. But Chekhov's stars, some as large as a goose's egg and some as small as hempseed, are still exactly where they were, in the sky of his story "Easter Eve." And from them to us that night still travels—for so much more than symbols, they are Chekhov looking at his sky.

Communication through fiction frequently happens, I believe, in ways that are small—a word is not too small; that are unannounced; that are less direct than we might first suppose on seeing how important they are. It isn't communication happening when you as the reader follow or predict the novel's plot or agree with, or anticipate, or could even quote the characters; when you hail the symbols; even when its whole landscape and climate have picked you up and transported you where it happens. But communication is going on, and regardless of all the rest, when you believe the writer.

Then is plausibility at the bottom of it? When we can read and say, "Oh, how right, I think so too," has the writer come through? Only stop to think how often simple plausibility, if put to measure a good story, falls down, while the story stands up, never wavers. And agreement isn't always, by any means, a mark of having been reached.

As a reader who never held a gun, I risk saying that it isn't exactly plausible that Old Ben, the bear in Faulkner's story, when he was finally brought down by a knife-thrust, had already in him fifty-two little hard lumps which were old bullets that had had no effect on him. Yet as a reader caught in the story, I think I qualify to bear witness that nothing less than fifty-two bullets could have been embedded in Old Ben or Old Ben he would not be. Old Ben and every one of his bullets along with him are parts of the truth in this story, William Faulkner's particular truth.

Belief doesn't depend on plausibility, but it seems to be a fact that validity of a kind, and this is of course a subjective kind, gained in whatever way that had to be, is the quality that makes a work reliable as art. This reliability comes straight out of the writer himself. In the end, it is another personal quotient in writing fiction; it is something inimitable. It is that by which each writer *lets us believe*— doesn't ask us to, can't make us, simply lets us.

To a large extent a writer cannot help the material of his fiction. That is, he cannot help where and when he happened to be born; then he has to live somewhere and somehow and with others, and survive through some history or other if he is here to write at all. But it is not to escape his life but more to pin it down that he writes fiction (though by pinning it down he no doubt does escape it a little). And so certainly he does choose his subject. It's not really quibbling to say that a writer's subject, in due time, chooses the writer—not of course *as* a writer, but as the man or woman who comes across it by living and has it to struggle with. That person may come on it by seeming accident, like falling over a chair in a dark room. But he may invite it with wide-open arms, so that it eventually walks in. Or his subject may accrue, build up and build up inside him until it's intolerable to him not to try to write it in terms he can understand: he submits it to the imagination, he finds names, sets something down. "In other words . . ."

So he does choose his subject, though not without compulsion, and now not too much stands in the way of the writer's learning something for himself about his own writing. For he has taken the fatal step when he put himself into his subject's hands. He might even do well to feel some misgivings: he and his fiction were never strangers, but at moments he may wonder at the ruthlessness of the relationship, which is honesty, between it and himself.

His inspiration, so-called, may very easily, then, be personal desperation—painful or pleasurable. All kinds of desperation get to be one in the work. But it will be the particular desperation that the particular writer is heir to, subject to, out of which he learns in daily life, by which, in that year, he is driven, on which he can feel, think, construct something, write out in as many drafts as he likes and then not get to much of an end. What he checks his work against remains, all the way, not books, not lore, neither another's writing nor in the large his own, but life that breathes in his face. Still, he may get to *his* end, have *his* say.

It really is his say. We have the writer's own vision of everything in the world when we place his novel in the center. Then so much is clear: how he sees life and death, how much he thinks people matter to each other and to themselves, how much he would like you to know what he finds beautiful or strange or awful or absurd, what he can do without, how well he has learned to see, hear, touch, smell—all as his sentences go by and in their time and sequence mount up. It grows clear how he imposes order and structure on his fictional world; and it is terribly clear, in the end, whether, when he calls for understanding, he gets any.

And of course he knew this would be so: he has been, and he is, a *reader.* Furthermore, all his past is in his point of view; his novel, whatever its subject, is the history itself of his life's experience in feeling. He has invited us, while we are his readers, to see with his point of view. Can we see? And what does he feel passionately about? Is it honest passion? The answer to that we know from the opening page. For some reason, honesty is one thing that it's almost impossible to make a mistake about in reading fiction.

Let us not think, however, that we ever plumb it all—not one whole novel; and I am not speaking of the great ones exclusively. It is for quite other reasons that we never know all of a single person. But the finished novel transcends the personal in art. Indeed, that has been its end in view.

For fiction, ideally, is highly personal but objective. It is something which only you can write but which is not, necessarily, *about* you. Style, I think, is whatever it is in the prose which has constantly pressed to give the writing its objectivity. Style does not obtrude but exists as the sum total of all the ways that have been taken to make the work stand on its own, apart. Born subjective, we learn what our own idea of the objective is as we go along.

Style is a product of highly conscious effort but is not self-conscious. Even with esthetic reasons aside, the self-consciousness would not be justified. For if you have worked in any serious way, you *have* your style—like the smoke from a fired cannon, like the ring in the water after the fish is pulled out or jumps back in. I can't see that a writer deserves praise in particular for his style, however good: in order for him to have written what he must have very much wanted to write, a way had to be found. A reader's understanding of his style—as the picture, or the reflection, or the proof of a way in which communication tried to happen—is more to be wished for than any praise;

and when communication does happen, the style is in effect beyond praise.

What you write about is in the public domain. Subject you can choose, but your mind and heart compel you. Point of view you develop in order to transcend it. Style you acquire in the pursuit of something else which may turn out to be the impossible. Now let me mention shape.

In fiction, as we know, the shapes the work takes are marvelous, and vary most marvelously in our minds. It is hard to speak further about them. Specific in the work, in the mind, but not describable anywhere else—or not by me; shape is something felt. It is the form of the work that you feel to be under way as you write and as you read. At the end, instead of farewell, it tells over the whole, as a whole, to the reader's memory.

In sculpture, this shape is left in rock itself and stands self-identifying and self-announcing. Fiction is made of words to travel under the reading eye, and made to go in one sequence and one direction, slowly, accumulating; time is an element. The words follow the contours of some continuous relationship between what can be told and what cannot be told, to be in the silence of reading the lightest of the hammers that tap their way along this side of chaos.

Fiction's progress is of course not tactile, though at once you might rejoin by saying that some of Lawrence's stories, for instance, *are*—as much as a stroke of the hand down a horse's neck. Neither is shape necessarily, or even often, formal, though James, for example, was so fond of making it so. There is no more limit to the kinds of shape a fictional work may take than there appears to be to the range and character of our minds.

The novel or story ended, shape must have made its own impression on the reader, so that he feels that some design in life (by which I mean esthetic pattern, not purpose) has just been discovered there. And this pattern, shape, form that emerges for you then, a reader at the end of the book, may do the greatest thing that fiction does: it may move you. And however you have been moved by the parts, this still has to happen from the whole before you know what indeed you have met with in that book.

From the writer's view, we might say that shape is most closely connected with the work itself, is the course it ran. From the reader's view, we might say that shape is connected with recognition; it is what allows us to know and remember what in the world of feeling we have been living through in that novel. The part of the mind in both reader and writer that form speaks to may be the deep-seated perception we all carry in us of the beauty of order imposed, of structure rising and building upon itself, and finally of this coming to rest.

It is through the shaping of the work in the hands of the artist that you most nearly come to know what can be known, on the page, of his mind and heart, and his as apart from the others. No other saw life in an ordering exactly like this. So shape begins and ends subjectively. And that the two concepts, writer's and reader's, may differ, since all of us differ, is neither so strange nor so important as the vital fact that a connection has been made between them. Our whole reading lives testify to the astonishing degree to which this can happen.

This ordering, or shape, a felt thing that emerges whole for us at the very last, as we close the novel to think back, was to the writer, I think, known first thing of all. It was surmised. And this is above all what nobody else knew or could have taught or told him. Besides, at that point he was not their listener. He could not, it seems, have cast his work except in the mold it's in, which was there in his mind all the hard way through. And this notwithstanding thousands of other things that life crowded into his head, parts of the characters that we shall never meet, flashes of action that yielded to other flashes, conversations drowned out, pieces of days and nights, all to be given up, and rightly.

For we have to remember what the novel is. Made by the imagination for the imagination, it is an illusion come full circle—a very exclusive thing, for all it seems to include a good deal of the world. It was wholly for the sake of illusion, made by art out of, and in order to show, and to be, some human truth, that the novelist took all he knew with him and made that leap in the dark.

For he must already have apprehended and come to his own jumping-off place before he could put down on paper that ever-miraculous thing, the opening sentence.

1965

Must the Novelist Crusade?

Not too long ago I read in some respectable press that Faulkner would have to be reassessed because he was "after all, only a white Mississippian." For this reason, it was felt, readers could no longer rely on him for knowing what he was writing about in his life's work of novels and stories, laid in what he called "my country."

Remembering how Faulkner for most of his life wrote in all but isolation from critical understanding, ignored impartially by North and South, with only a handful of critics in forty years who were able to "assess" him, we might smile at this journalist as at a boy let out of school. Or there may have been an instinct to smash the superior, the good, that is endurable enough to go on offering itself. But I feel in these words and others like them the agonizing of our times. I think they come of an honest and understandable zeal to allot every writer his chance to better the world or go to his grave reproached for the mess it is in. And here, it seems to me, the heart of fiction's real reliability has been struck at—and not for the first time by the noble hand of the crusader.

It would not be surprising if the critic I quote had gained his knowledge of the South from the books of the author he repudiates. At any rate, a reply to him exists there. Full evidence as to whether any writer, alive or dead, can be believed is always at hand in one place: any page of his work. The color of his skin would modify it just about as much as would the binding of his book. Integrity can be neither lost nor concealed nor faked nor quenched nor artificially come by nor outlived, nor, I believe, in the long run denied. Integrity is no greater and no less today than it was yesterday and will be tomorrow. It stands outside time.

The novelist and the crusader who writes both have their own place—in the novel and the editorial respectively, equally valid whether or not the two happen to be in agreement. In my own view, writing fiction places the novelist and the crusader on opposite sides. But they are not the sides of right and wrong. Honesty is not at stake here and is not questioned; the only thing at stake is the proper use of words for the proper ends. And a mighty thing it is.

Because the printed page is where the writer's work is to be seen, it may be natural for people who do not normally read fiction to confuse novels with journalism or speeches. The very using of words has these well-intentioned people confused about the novelist's purpose.

The writing of a novel is taking life as it already exists, not to report it but to make an object, toward the end that the finished work might contain this life inside it, and offer it to the reader. The essence will not be, of course, the same thing as the raw material; it is not even of the same family of things. The novel is something that never was before and will not be again. For the mind of one person, its writer, is in it too. What distinguishes it above all from the raw material, and what distinguishes it from journalism, is that inherent in the novel is the possibility of a shared act of the imagination between its writer and its reader.

"All right, Eudora Welty, what are you going to do about it? Sit down there with your mouth shut?" asked a stranger over long distance in one of the midnight calls that I suppose have waked most writers in the South from time to time. It is part of the same question: Are fiction writers on call to be crusaders? For us in the South who are fiction writers, is writing a novel *something we can do about it?*

It can be said at once, I should think, that we are all agreed upon the most important point: that morality as shown through human relationships is the whole heart of fiction, and the serious writer has never lived who dealt with anything else.

And yet, the zeal to reform, which quite properly inspires the editorial, has never done fiction much good. The exception occurs when it can rise to the intensity of satire, where it finds a better home in the poem or the drama. Large helpings of naïveté and self-esteem, which serve to refresh the crusader, only encumber the novelist. How unfair it is that when a novel is to be written, it is never enough to have our hearts in the right place! But good will all by itself can no more get a good novel written than it can paint in watercolor or sing Mozart.

Nevertheless, let us suppose that we feel we might help if we were to write a crusading novel. What will our problems be?

Before anything else, speed. The crusader's message is

prompted by crisis; it has to be delivered on time. Suppose John Steinbeck had only now finished *The Grapes of Wrath?* The ordinary novelist has only one message: "I submit that this is one way we are." This can wait. When we think of Ibsen, we see that causes themselves may in time be forgotten, their championship no longer needed; it is Ibsen's passion that keeps the plays alive.

Next, we as the crusader-novelist shall find awkward to use the very weapon we count on most: the generality. On fiction's pages, generalities clank when wielded, and hit with equal force at the little and the big, at the merely suspect and the really dangerous. They make too much noise for us to hear what people might be trying to say. They are fatal to tenderness and are in themselves non-conductors of any real, however modest, discovery of the writer's own heart. This discovery is the best hope of the ordinary novelist, and to make it he begins not with the generality but with the particular in front of his eyes, which he is able to examine.

Taking a particular situation existing in his world, and what he feels about it in his own breast and what he can make of it in his own head, he constructs on paper, little by little, an equivalent of it. Literally it may correspond to a high degree or to none at all; emotionally it corresponds as closely as he can make it. Observation and the inner truth of that observation as he perceives it, the two being tested one against the other: to him this is what the writing of a novel is.

We, the crusader-novelist, having started with our generality, must end with a generality; they had better be the same. In the place of climax, we can deliver a judgment. How can the plot seem disappointing when it is a lovely argument spread out? It is because fiction is stone-deaf to argument.

The ordinary novelist does not argue; he hopes to show, to disclose. His persuasions are all toward allowing his reader to see and hear something for himself. He knows another bad thing about arguments: they carry the menace of neatness into fiction. Indeed, what we as the crusader-novelist are scared of most is confusion.

Great fiction, we very much fear, abounds in what makes for confusion; it generates it, being on a scale which copies life, which it confronts. It is very seldom neat, is given to sprawling and escaping from bounds, is capable of contradicting itself, and is not impervious to humor. There is absolutely everything in great fiction but a clear answer. Humanity itself seems to matter more to the novelist than what humanity thinks it can prove.

When a novelist writes of man's experience, what else is he to draw on but the life around him? And yet the life around him, on the surface, can be used to show anything, absolutely anything, as readers know. The novelist's real task and real responsibility lie in the way he uses it.

Situation itself always exists; it is whatever life is up to here and now, it is the living and present moment. It is transient, and it fluctuates. Using the situation, the writer populates his novel with characters invented to express it in their terms.

It is important that it be in their terms. We cannot in fiction set people to acting mechanically or carrying placards to make their sentiments plain. People are not Right and Wrong, Good and Bad, Black and White personified; flesh and blood and the sense of comedy object. Fiction writers cannot be tempted to make the mistake of looking at people in the generality—that is to say, of seeing people as not at all *like us*. If human beings are to be comprehended as real, then they have to be treated as real, with minds, hearts, memories, habits, hopes, with passions and capacities like ours. This is why novelists begin the study of people from within.

The first act of insight is throw away the labels. In fiction, while we do not necessarily write about ourselves, we write out of ourselves, using ourselves; what we learn from, what we are sensitive to, what we feel strongly about—these become our characters and go to make our plots. Characters in fiction are conceived from within, and they have, accordingly, their own interior life; they are individuals every time. The character we care about in a novel we may not approve of or agree with—that's beside the point. But he has got to seem alive. Then and only then, when we read, we experience or surmise things about life itself that are deeper and more lasting and less destructive to understanding than approval or disapproval.

The novelist's work is highly organized, but I should say it is organized around anything but logic. Just as characters are not labels but are made from the inside out and grow into their own life, so does a plot have a living principle on which it hangs together and gradually earns its shape. A plot is a thousand times more unsettling than an argument, which may be answered. It is not a pattern imposed; it is inward emotion acted out. It is arbitrary, indeed, but not artificial. It is possibly so odd that it might be called a vision, but it is organic to its material: it is a working vision, then.

A writer works *through* what is around him if he wishes to get to what he is after—no kind of proof, but simply an essence. In practice he will do anything at all with his material: shape it, strain it to the breaking point, double it up, or use it backward; he will balk at nothing—see *The Sound and the Fury*—to reach that heart and core. But even in a good cause he does not falsify it. The material itself receives deep ultimate respect: it has given rise to the vision of it, which in turn has determined what the novel shall be.

The ordinary novelist, who can never make a perfect thing, can with every novel try again. But if we write a novel to prove something, one novel will settle it, for why prove a thing more than once? And what, then, is to keep all novels by all right-thinking persons from being pretty much alike? Or exactly alike? There would be little reason for present writers to keep on, no reason for the new writers to start. There's no way to know, but we might guess that the reason the young write no fiction behind the Iron Curtain is the obvious fact that to be acceptable there, all novels must conform, and so must be alike, hence valueless. If the personal vision can be made to order, then we should lose, writer and reader alike, our own gift for perceiving, seeing through the fabric of everyday to what to each pair of eyes on earth is a unique thing. We'd accept life exactly like everybody else, and so, of course, be content with it. We should not even miss our vanished novelists. And if life ever became not worth writing fiction about, that, I believe, would be the first sign that it wasn't worth living.

With a blueprint to work with instead of a vision, there is a good deal that we as the crusader-novelist must be at pains to leave out. Unavoidably, I think, we shall leave out one of the greatest things. This is the mystery in life. Our blueprint for sanity and of solution for trouble leaves out the dark. (This is odd, because surely it was the dark that first troubled us.) We leave out the wonder because with wonder it is impossible to argue, much less to settle. The ordinary novelist thinks it had better be recognized. Reckless as this may make him, he believes the insoluble is part of his material too.

The novelist works neither to correct nor to condone, not at all to comfort, but to make what's told alive. He assumes at the start an enlightenment in his reader equal to his own, for they are hopefully on the point of taking off together from that base into the rather different world of the imagination.

It's not only the fact that this world is bigger and that fewer constrictions apply that may daunt us as crusaders. But the imagination itself is the problem. It is capable of saying everything but no. In our literature, what has traveled the longest way through time is the great affirmative soul of Chaucer. The novel itself always affirms, it seems to me, by the nature of itself. It says what people are like. It doesn't, and doesn't know how to, describe what they are *not* like, and it would waste its time if it told us what we ought to be like, since we already know that, don't we? But we may not know nearly so well what we are as when a novel of power reveals this to us. For the first time we may, as we read, see ourselves in our own situation, in some curious way reflected. By whatever way the novelist accomplishes it—there are many ways—truth is borne in on us in all its great weight and angelic lightness, and accepted as home truth.

Passing judgment on his fellows, which is trying enough for anybody, is frustrating for an author. It is hardly the way to make the discoveries about living that he must have hoped for when he began to write. If he does not pass judgment, does this mean he has no conscience? Of course he has a conscience; it is, like his temperament, his own, and he is one hundred percent answerable to it, whether it is convenient or not. What matters is that a writer is committed to his own moral principles. If he is, when we read him we cannot help but be aware of what these are. Certainly the characters of his novel and the plot they move in are their ultimate reflections. But these convictions are implicit; they are deep down; they are the rock on which the whole structure of more than that novel rests.

Indeed, we are more aware of his moral convictions through a novel than any flat statement of belief from him could make us. We are aware in that part of our mind that tells us truths about ourselves. Yet it is only by way of the imagination—the novelist's to ours—that such private neighborhoods are reached.

There is still to mention what I think will give us, as the crusader-novelist, the hardest time: our voice will not be our own. The crusader's voice is the voice of the crowd and must rise louder all the time, for there is, of course, the other side to be drowned out. Worse, the voices of most crowds sound alike. Worse still, the voice that seeks to do other than communicate when it makes a noise has something brutal about it; it is no longer using words as words but as something to brandish, with which to threaten, brag or condemn. The noise is the simple assertion of self, the great, mindless, general self. And for all its volume it is ephemeral. Only meaning lasts. Nothing was ever learned in a crowd, from a crowd, or by addressing or trying to please a crowd. Even to deplore, yelling is out of place. To deplore a thing as hideous as the murder of the three civil rights workers demands the quiet in which to absorb it.

Enormities can be lessened, cheapened, just as good and delicate things can be. We can and will cheapen all feeling by letting it go savage or parading in it.

Writing fiction is an interior affair. Novels and stories always will be put down little by little out of personal feeling and personal beliefs arrived at alone and at firsthand over a period of time as time is needed. To go outside and beat the drum is only to interrupt, interrupt, and so finally to forget and to lose. Fiction has, and must keep, a private address. For life is *lived* in a private place; where it means anything is inside the mind and heart. Fiction has always shown life where it is lived, and good fiction, or so I have faith, will continue to do this.

A Passage to India is an old novel now. It is an intensely moral novel. It deals with race prejudice. Mr. Forster, not by preaching at us, while being passionately concerned, makes us know his points unforgettably as often as we read it. And does he not bring in the dark! The points are good forty years after their day *because of the splendor of the novel.* What a lesser novelist's harangues would have buried by now, his imagination still reveals. Revelation of even the strongest forces is delicate work.

Indeed, great fiction shows us not how to conduct our behavior but how to feel. Eventually, it may show us how to face our feelings and face our actions and to have new inklings about what they mean. A good novel of any year can initiate us into our own new experience.

From the working point of view of the serious writer of fiction, nothing has changed today but the externals. They are important externals; we may have developed an increased awareness of them, which is certainly to the good;

we have at least the same capacity as ever for understanding, the same eyes and ears, same hearts to feel, same minds to agonize or remember or to try to put things together, see things in proportion with. While the raw material of our fiction is changing dramatically—as indeed it is changing everywhere—we are the same instruments of perceiving that we ever were. I should not trust us if we were not. And we do not know what is to be made out of experience at any time until the personal quotient has been added. To convey what we see around us, whatever it is, so as to let it speak for itself according to our lights is the same challenge it ever was, not a different one, not a greater one, only perhaps made harder by the times. Now as ever we must keep writing from what we know; and we must really know it.

No matter how fast society around us changes, what remains is that there is a relationship in progress between ourselves and other people; this was the case when the world seemed stable, too. There are relationships of the blood, of the passions and the affections, of thought and spirit and deed. There is the relationship between the races. How can one kind of relationship be set apart from the others? Like the great root system of an old and long-established growing plant, they are all tangled up together; to separate them you would have to cleave the plant itself from top to bottom.

What must the Southern writer of fiction do today? Shall he do anything different from what he has always done?

There have already been giant events, some of them wrenchingly painful and humiliating. And now there is added the atmosphere of hate. We in the South are a hated people these days; we were hated first for actual and particular reasons, and now we may be hated still more in some vast unparticularized way. I believe there must be such a thing as sentimental hate. Our people hate back.

I think the worst of it is we are getting stuck in it. We are like trapped flies with our feet not in honey but in venom. It's not love that is the gluey emotion; it's hate. As far as writing goes, which is as far as living goes, this is a devastating emotion. It could kill us. This hate seems in part shame for self, in part self-justification, in part panic that life is really changing.

Fury at ourselves and hurt pride, anger aroused too often, outrage at being hated need not obscure forever the sore spots we Southerners know better than our detractors. For some of us have shown bad hearts. As in the case of our better qualities, we are locally blessed with an understanding and intimate knowledge of our faults that our worst detractors cannot match, and have been in a less relentless day far more relentless, more eloquent, too, than they have yet learned to be.

I do not presume to speak for my fellow Southern writers, a group of individuals if there ever was one. Yet I would like to point something out: in the rest of the country people seem suddenly aware now of what Southern fiction writers have been writing about in various ways for a great long time. We do not need reminding of what our subject is. It is humankind, and we are all part of it. When we write about people, black or white, in the South or anywhere, if our stories are worth the reading, we are writing about everybody.

In the South, we who are now at work may not learn to write it before we learn, or learn again, to live it—our full life in the South within its context, in its relation to the rest of the world. "Only connect," Forster's ever wise and gentle and daring words, could be said to us in our homeland quite literally at this moment. And while the Southern writer goes on portraying his South, which I think nobody else can do and which I believe he must do, then if his work is done well enough, it will reflect a larger mankind as it has done before.

And so finally I think we need to write with love. Not in self-defense, not in hate, not in the mood of instruction, not in rebuttal, in any kind of militance, or in apology, but with love. Not in exorcisement, either, for this is to make the reader bear a thing for you.

Neither do I speak of writing forgivingly; out of love you can write with straight fury. It is the *source* of the understanding that I speak of; it's this that determines its nature and its reach.

We are told that Turgenev's nostalgic, profoundly reflective, sensuously alive stories that grew out of his memories of early years reached the Czar and were given some credit by him when he felt moved to free the serfs in Russia. Had Turgenev set out to write inflammatory tracts instead of the sum of all he knew, could express, of life learned at firsthand, how much less of his mind and heart with their commitments, all implicit, would have filled his stories! But he might be one of us now, so directly are we touched with a hundred and thirteen years gone by since they were first published.

Indifference would indeed be corrupting to the fiction writer, indifference to any part of man's plight. Passion is the chief ingredient of good fiction. It flames right out of sympathy for the human condition and goes into all great writing. (And of course passion and the temper are different things; writing in the heat of passion can be done with extremely good temper.) But to distort a work of passion for the sake of a cause is to cheat, and the end, far from justifying the means, is fairly sure to be lost with it. Then the novel will have been not the work of imagination, at once passionate and objective, made by a man struggling in solitude with something of his own to say, but a piece of catering.

To cater to is not to love and not to serve well either. We do need to bring to our writing, over and over again, all the abundance we possess. To be able, to be ready, to enter into the minds and hearts of our own people, all of them, to comprehend them (us) and then to make characters and plots in stories that in honesty and with honesty reveal them (ourselves) to us, in whatever situation we live through in our own times: this is the continuing job, and it's no harder now than it ever was, I suppose. Every writer, like everybody else, thinks he's living through the crisis of the ages. To write honestly and with all our powers is the least we can do, and the most.

Time, though it can make happenings and trappings out of date, cannot do much to change the realities apprehended by the imagination. History will change in Mississippi, and the hope is that it will change in a beneficial direction and with a merciful speed, and above all bring insight, understanding. But when William Faulkner's novels come to be pictures of a society that is no more, they will still be good and still be authentic because of what went into them from the man himself. Mankind still tries the same things and suffers the same falls, climbs up to try again, and novels are as true at one time as at another. Love and hate, hope and despair, justice and injustice, compassion and prejudice, truth-telling and lying work in all men; their story can be told in whatever skin they are wearing and in whatever year the writer can put them down.

Faulkner is not receding from us. Indeed, his work, though it can't increase in itself, increases us. His work throws light on the past and on today as it becomes the past—the day in its journey. This being so, it informs the future too.

What is written in the South from now on is going to be taken into account by Faulkner's work; I mean the remark literally. Once Faulkner had written, we could never unknow what he told us and showed us. And his work will do the same thing tomorrow. We inherit from him, while we can get fresh and firsthand news of ourselves from his work at any time.

A source of illumination is not dated by what passes along under its ray, is not qualified or disqualified by the nature of the traffic. When the light of Faulkner's work will be discovering things to us no more, it will be discovering *us*. Even we shall lie enfolded in perspective one day: what we hoped along with what we did, what we didn't do, and not only what we were but what we missed being, what others yet to come might dare to be. For we *are* our own crusade. Before ever we write, we are. Instead of our judging Faulkner, he will be revealing us in books to later minds.

1965

"Is Phoenix Jackson's Grandson Really Dead?"

A story writer is more than happy to be read by students; the fact that these serious readers think and feel something in response to his work he finds life-giving. At the same time he may not always be able to reply to their specific questions in kind. I wondered if it might clarify something, for both the questioners and myself, if I set down a general reply to the question that comes to me most often in the mail, from both students and their teachers, after some classroom discussion. The unrivaled favorite is this: "Is Phoenix Jackson's grandson really *dead*?"

It refers to a short story I wrote years ago called "A Worn Path," which tells of a day's journey an old woman makes on foot from deep in the country into town and into a doctor's office on behalf of her little grandson; he is at home, periodically ill, and periodically she comes for his medicine; they give it to her as usual, she receives it and starts the journey back.

I had not meant to mystify readers by withholding any

fact; it is not a writer's business to tease. The story is told through Phoenix's mind as she undertakes her errand. As the author at one with the character as I tell it, I must assume that the boy is alive. As the reader, you are free to think as you like, of course: the story invites you to believe that no matter what happens, Phoenix for as long as she is able to walk and can hold to her purpose will make her journey. The *possibility* that she would keep on even if he were dead is there in her devotion and its single-minded, single-track errand. Certainly the *artistic* truth, which should be good enough for the fact, lies in Phoenix's own answer to that question. When the nurse asks, "He isn't dead, is he?" she speaks for herself: "He still the same. He going to last."

The grandchild is the incentive. But it is the journey, the going of the errand, that is the story, and the question is not whether the grandchild is in reality alive or dead. It doesn't affect the outcome of the story or its meaning from start to finish. But it is not the question itself that has struck me as much as the idea, almost without exception implied in the asking, that for Phoenix's grandson to be dead would somehow make the story "better."

It's *all right*, I want to say to the students who write to me, for things to be what they appear to be, and for words to mean what they say. It's all right, too, for words and appearances to mean more than one thing—ambiguity is a fact of life. A fiction writer's responsibility covers not only what he presents as the facts of a given story but what he chooses to stir up as their implications; in the end, these implications, too, become facts, in the larger, fictional sense. But it is not all right, not in good faith, for things *not* to mean what they say.

The grandson's plight was real and it made the truth of the story, which is the story of an errand of love carried out. If the child no longer lived, the truth would persist in the "wornness" of the path. But his being dead can't increase the truth of the story, can't affect it one way or the other. I think I signal this, because the end of the story has been reached before old Phoenix gets home again: she simply starts back. To the question "Is the grandson really dead?" I could reply that it doesn't make any difference. I could also say that I did not make him up in order to let him play a trick on Phoenix. But my best answer would be: "*Phoenix* is alive."

The origin of a story is sometimes a trustworthy clue to the author—or can provide him with the clue—to its key image; maybe in this case it will do the same for the reader. One day I saw a solitary old woman like Phoenix. She was walking; I saw her, at middle distance, in a winter country landscape, and watched her slowly make her way across my line of vision. That sight of her made me write the story. I invented an errand for her, but that only seemed a living part of the figure she was herself: what errand other than for someone else could be making her go? And her going was the first thing, her persisting in her landscape was the real thing, and the first and the real were what I wanted and worked to keep. I brought her up close enough, by imagination, to describe her face, make her present to the eyes, but the full-length figure moving across the winter fields was the indelible one and the image to keep, and the perspective extending into the vanishing distance the true one to hold in mind.

I invented for my character, as I wrote, some passing adventures—some dreams and harassments and a small triumph or two, some jolts to her pride, some flights of fancy to console her, one or two encounters to scare her, a moment that gave her cause to feel ashamed, a moment to dance and preen—for it had to be a *journey*, and all these things belonged to that, parts of life's uncertainty.

A narrative line is in its deeper sense, of course, the tracing out of a meaning, and the real continuity of a story lies in this probing forward. The real dramatic force of a story depends on the strength of the emotion that has set it going. The emotional value is the measure of the reach of the story. What gives any such content to "A Worn Path" is not its circumstances but its *subject*: the deep-grained habit of love.

What I hoped would come clear was that in the whole surround of this story, the world it threads through, the only certain thing at all is the worn path. The habit of love cuts through confusion and stumbles or contrives its way out of difficulty, it remembers the way even when it forgets, for a dumbfounded moment, its reason for being. The path is the thing that matters.

Her victory—old Phoenix's—is when she sees the diploma in the doctor's office, when she finds "nailed up on the wall the document that had been stamped with the gold seal and framed in the gold frame, which matched the dream that was hung up in her head." The return with the medicine is just a matter of retracing her own footsteps. It is the part of the journey, and of the story, that can now go without saying.

In the matter of function, old Phoenix's way might even do as a sort of parallel to your way of work if you are a writer of stories. The way to get there is the all-important, all-absorbing problem, and this problem is your reason for undertaking the story. Your only guide, too, is your sureness about your subject, about what this subject is. Like Phoenix, you work all your life to find your way, through all the obstructions and the false appearances and the upsets you may have brought on yourself, to reach a meaning—using inventions of your imagination, perhaps helped out by your dreams and bits of good luck. And finally too, like Phoenix, you have to assume that what you are working in aid of is life, not death.

But you would make the trip anyway—wouldn't you?—just on hope.

1974

Some Notes on Time in Fiction

Time and place, the two bases of reference upon which the novel, in seeking to come to grips with human experience, must depend for its validity, operate together, of course. They might be taken for granted as ordinary factors, until the novelist at his work comes to scrutinize them apart.

Place, the accessible one, the inhabited one, has blessed identity—a proper name, a human history, a visible character. Time is anonymous; when we give it a face, it's the same face the world over. While place is in itself as informing as an old gossip, time tells us nothing about itself except by the signals that it is passing. It has never given anything away.

Unlike time, place has surface, which will take the imprint of man—his hand, his foot, his mind; it can be tamed, domesticized. It has shape, size, boundaries; man can measure himself against them. It has atmosphere and temperature, change of light and show of season, qualities to which man spontaneously responds. Place has always nursed, nourished and instructed man; he in turn can rule it and ruin it, take it and lose it, suffer if he is exiled from it, and after living on it he goes to it in his grave. It is the stuff of fiction, as close to our living lives as the earth we can pick up and rub between our fingers, something we can feel and smell. But time is like the wind of the abstract. Beyond its all-pervasiveness, it has no quality that we apprehend but rate of speed, and our own acts and thoughts are said to give it that. Man can feel love for place; he is prone to regard time as something of an enemy.

Yet the novelist lives on closer terms with time than he does with place. The reasons for this are much older than any novel; they reach back into our oldest lore. How many of our proverbs are little nutshells to pack the meat of time in! ("He that diggeth a pit shall fall into it." "Pride goeth before destruction, and a haughty spirit before a fall.") The all-withstanding devices of myth and legend (the riddle of the Sphinx, Penelope's web, the Thousand and One Nights) are constructed of time. And time goes to make that most central device of all, the plot itself—as Scheherazade showed us in her own telling.

Indeed, these little ingots of time are ingots of plot too. Not only do they contain stories, they convey the stories— they speak of life-in-the-movement, with a beginning and an end. All that needed to be added was the middle; then the novel came along and saw to that.

Only the nursery fairy tale is not answerable to time, and time has no effect upon it; time winds up like a toy, and toy it is: when set to "Once upon a time" it spins till it runs down at "Happy ever after." Fairy tales don't come from old wisdom, they come from old foolishness—just as potent. They follow rules of their own that are quite as strict as time's (the magic of number and repetition, the governing of the spell); their fairy perfection forbids the existence of choices, and the telling always has to be the same. Their listener is the child, whose gratification comes of the fairy tale's having no suspense. The tale is about wishes, and thus grants a wish itself.

Real life is not wished, it is lived; stories and novels, whose subject is human beings in relationship with experience to undergo, make their own difficult way, struggle toward their own resolutions. Instead of fairy immunity to change, there is the vulnerability of human imperfection caught up in human emotion, and so there is growth, there is crisis, there is fulfillment, there is decay. Life moves toward death. The novel's progress is one of causality, and with that comes suspense. Suspense is a necessity in a novel because it is a main condition of our existence. Suspense is known only to mortals, and its agent and messenger is time.

The novel is time's child—"I could a tale *unfold*"—and bears all the earmarks, and all the consequences.

The novelist can never do otherwise than work with time, and nothing in his novel can escape it. The novel cannot begin without his starting of the clock; the characters then, and not until then, are seen to be alive, in motion; their situation can declare itself only by its unfolding. While place lies passive, time moves and is a mover. Time is the bringer-on of action, the instrument of change. If time should break down, the novel itself would lie in collapse, its meaning gone. For time has the closest possible connection with the novel's meaning, in being the chief conductor of the plot.

Thus time is not a simple length, on which to string beadlike the novel's episodes. Though it does join acts and events in a row, it's truer to say that it leads them in a direction, it induces each one out of the one before and into the one next. It is not only the story's "then—and then," it may also be a "but" or a "nevertheless"; and it is always a "thus" and a "therefore."

Why does a man do a certain thing now, what in the past has brought him to it, what in the future will come of it, and into what sequence will he set things moving now? Time, in which the characters behave and perform, alone and with others, through the changes rung by their situation, uncovers motive and develops the consequences. Time carries out a role of resolver. ("As a man soweth, so shall he reap.")

Clock time has an arbitrary, bullying power over daily affairs that of course can't be got around (the Mad Hatter's tea party). But it has not the same power in fiction that it has in life. Time is plot's right arm, indeed, but is always answerable to it. It can act only in accordance with the plot, lead only toward the plot's development and fulfillment.

Fiction does not hesitate to accelerate time, slow it down, project it forward or run it backward, cause it to skip over itself or repeat itself. It may require time to travel in a circle, to meet itself in coincidence. It can freeze an action in the middle of its performance. It can expand a single moment like the skin of a balloon or bite off a life like a thread. It can put time through the hoop of a dream, trap it inside an obsession. It can set a fragment of the past within a frame of the present and cause them to exist simultaneously. In Katherine Anne Porter's perfect short story

"The Grave," a forgotten incident from her country-Texas childhood abruptly projects itself upon a woman's present; its meaning—too deep for the child's understanding— travels twenty years through time and strikes her full force on a city street in another country. In this story, time moves by metamorphosis, and in the flash it discloses another, earlier metamorphosis—the real one, which had lain there all the while in the past that the young woman had left behind her.

In going in the direction of meaning, time has to move through a mind. What it will bring about is an awakening there. Through whatever motions it goes through, it will call forth, in a mind or heart, some crucial recognition. ("I imagined that I bore my chalice safely through a throng of foes.")

What can a character come to know, of himself and others, by working through a given situation? This is what fiction asks, with an emotional urgency driving it all the way; and can he know it in time? Thus time becomes, as sharply as needed, an instrument of pressure. Any novel's situation must constitute some version of a matter of life or death. In the face of time, life is always at stake. This may or may not be the case in a literal sense; but it does need to be always the case as a matter of spiritual or moral survival. It may lie not so much in being rescued as in having learned what constitutes one's own danger, and one's own salvation. With the refinements of the danger involved, suspense is increased. Suspense has exactly the value of its own meaning.

In fiction, then, time can throb like a pulse, tick like a bomb, beat like the waves of a rising tide against the shore; it can be made out as the whisper of attrition, or come to an end with the explosion of a gun. For time is of course subjective, too. ("It tolls for thee.")

Time appears to do all these things in novels, but they are *effects*, necessary illusions performed by the novelist; and they make no alteration in the pace of the novel, which is one of a uniform steadiness and imperturbability. The novel might be told episodically, hovering over one section of time and skipping over the next; or by some eccentric method—Henry Green spoke of his as going crabwise; but however its style of moving, its own advance must remain smooth and unbroken, its own time all of a piece. The plot goes forward at the pace of its own necessity, its own heartbeat. Its way ahead, its line of meaning, is kept clear and unsnarled, stretched tight as a tuned string.

Time in a novel is the course through which, and by which, all things in their turn are brought forth in their significance—events, emotions, relationships in their changes, in their synchronized move toward resolution. It provides the order for the dramatic unfolding of the plot: revelation is not revelation until it is dramatically conceived and carried out.

The close three-way alliance of time, plot and significance can be seen clearly demonstrated in the well-written detective novel. We can learn from it that plot, by the very strength, spareness and boldness of its construction-in-motion, forms a kind of metaphor. I believe every well-made plot does, and needs to do so. But a living metaphor. From the simplest to the most awesomely complicated, a plot is a device organic to human struggle designed for the searching out of human truth. It is from inception highly sensitive to time, it acts within time, and it is in its time that we ourselves see it and follow it.

———

As readers, we accept more or less without blinking the novel's playing-free with time. Don't we by familiar practice accept discrepancies much like them in daily living? Fictional time bears a not too curious resemblance to our own interior clock; it is so by design. Fiction penetrates chronological time to reach our deeper version of time that's given to us by the way we think and feel. This is one of the reasons why even the first "stream-of-consciousness" novels, difficult as they must have been for their authors breaking new ground, were rather contrarily easy for the reader to follow.

Fictional time may be more congenial to us than clock time, precisely for human reasons. An awareness of time goes with us all our lives. Watch or no watch, we carry the awareness with us. It lies so deep, in the very grain of our characters, that who knows if it isn't as singular to each of us as our thumbprints. In the sense of our own transience may lie the one irreducible urgency telling us to do, to understand, to love.

We are mortal: this is time's deepest meaning in the novel as it is to us alive. Fiction shows us the past as well as the present moment in mortal light; it is an art served by the indelibility of our memory, and one empowered by a sharp and prophetic awareness of what is ephemeral. It is by the ephemeral that our feeling is so strongly aroused for what endures, or strives to endure. One time compellingly calls up the other. Thus the ephemeral, being alive only in the present moment, must be made to live in the novel as *now*, while it transpires, in the transpiring.

Fiction's concern is with the ephemeral—that is, the

human—effects of time, these alone. In action, scene and metaphor, these are set how unforgettably before our eyes! I believe the images of time may be the most indelible that fiction's art can produce. Miss Havisham's table in its spider-webs still laid for her wedding feast; the "certain airs" in *To the Lighthouse* that "fumbled the petals of roses"—they come instantaneously to mind. And do you not see the movement of Gusev's body in the sea, after his burial from the hospital ship: see it go below the surface of the sea, moving on down and swaying rhythmically with the current, and then being met by the shark: "After playing a little with the body the shark nonchalantly puts its jaws under it, cautiously touches it with its teeth, and the sail-cloth is rent its full length from head to foot." "Was it possible that such a thing might happen to anyone?" is the question Chekhov has asked as Gusev was slid into the sea, and in this chilling moment we look upon the story's answer, and we see not simply an act taking place in time; we are made, as witnesses, to see time happen. We look upon its answer as it occurs in time. This moment, this *rending*, is what might happen to anyone.

When passion comes into the telling, with a quickening of human meaning, changes take place in fictional time. Some of them are formidable.

I was recently lent a book by a student which had set itself to clear up *The Sound and the Fury* by means of a timetable; the characters' arrivals and departures, including births and deaths, were listed in schedule, with connections to and from the main points of action in the novel. What has defeated the compiler is that *The Sound and the*

Fury remains, after his work as before it, approachable only as a novel. He was right, of course, in seeing time to be at the bottom of it. Time, though—not chronology.

Think of the timepieces alone. Think of only one time-piece: Dilsey has to use the Compson clock; it has only one hand. "The clock tick-tocked, solemn and profound. It might have been the dry pulse of the decaying house itself; after a while it whirred and cleared its throat and struck." It strikes five times. "Eight o'clock," says Dilsey. Even while the clock is striking, chronology is in the act of yielding to another sort of time.

Through the telling of the story three times in succession by three different Compsons in the first-person and then once again in the third-person, we are exposed to three different worlds of memory, each moving in its own orbit. "He thirty-three," Luster says of Benjy, "thirty-three this morning," and the reply comes, "You mean he been three years old thirty years." Benjy's memory is involuntary and not conscious of sequence or connections: a stick run along the palings of a fence. But time of whatever nature leaves a residue in passing, and out of Benjy comes a wail "hopeless and prolonged. It was nothing. Just sound. It might have been all time and injustice and sorrow become vocal for an instant by a conjunction of planets."

Time to Quentin is visible—his shadow; is audible—his grandfather's watch; and it is the heavy load that has to be carried inside him—his memory. Excruciatingly conscious, possessing him in torture, that memory works in spite of him and of all he can do, anywhere he can go, this last day of his life. The particular moment in time that links him forever to the past—his world—conditions *all* time. The future may be an extension of the past *where pos-*

sible; the future can include memory *if bearable.* But time will repeatedly assault what has been intact; which may be as frail as the virginity of Caddy. If experience is now, at every stage, a tragedy of association in the memory, how is the rememberer to survive? Quentin spends his last day, as he's spent his life, answering that he is already dead. He has willed the past some quality, some power, by which it can arrest the present, try to stop it from happening; can stop it.

Who, in the swirling time of this novel, knows the actual time, and can tell the story by it? Jason, of course. He keeps track of time to the second as he keeps track of money to the penny. Time is money, says Jason. And he cheats on both and is in turn cheated by both; we see him at the end a man "sitting quietly behind the wheel of a small car, with his invisible life ravelled out about him like a worn-out sock."

By all the interior evidence, we will come nearest to an understanding of this novel through the ways it speaks to us out of its total saturation with time. We read not in spite of the eccentric handling of time, but as well as we can by the aid of it. If a point is reached in fiction where chronology has to be torn down, it must be in order to admit and make room for what matters overwhelmingly more to the human beings who are its characters.

Faulkner has crowded chronology out of the way many times to make way for memory and the life of the past, as we know, and we know for what reason. "Memory believes before knowing remembers," he says (in *Light in August*). Remembering is so basic and vital a part of staying alive that it takes on the strength of an instinct of survival, and acquires the power of an art. Remembering is done through the blood, it is a bequeathment, it takes account of what happens before a man is born as if he were there taking part. It is a physical absorption through the living body, it is a spiritual heritage. It is also a life's work.

"There is no such thing as was," Faulkner remarked in answer to a student's question as to why he wrote long sentences. "To me, no man is himself, he is the sum of his past. There is no such thing really as was, because the past is. It is a part of every man, every woman, and every moment. All of his and her ancestry, background, is all a part of himself and herself at any moment. And so a man, a character in a story at any moment in action, is not just himself as he is then, he is all that made him; and the long sentence," he adds, "is an attempt to get his past and possibly his future into the instant in which he does something..."

Distortion of time is a deeply conscious part of any novel's conception, is an organic part of its dramatic procedure, and throughout the novel's course it matters continuously and increasingly, and exactly as the author gives it to us. The dilations, the freezing of moments, the persistent recurrences and proliferations, all the extraordinary tamperings with time in *The Sound and the Fury,* are answers to the meaning's questions, evolving on demand. For all Faulkner does to chronological time here—he explodes it—he does nothing that does not increase the dramatic power of his story. The distortions to time give the novel its deepest seriousness of meaning, and charge it with an intense emotional power that could come from nowhere else. Time, in the result, is the living essence of *The Sound and the Fury.* It appears to stand so extremely close to the plot that, in a most extraordinary way, it almost becomes the plot itself. It *is* the portentous part; it is the plot's long reverberation. Time has taken us through every degree of the long down-spiral to the novel's meaning—into the meaning; it has penetrated its way. It has searched out every convolution of a human predicament and brought us to the findings of tragedy.

Faulkner's work is, we know, magnetized to a core of time, to his conception of it as the continuing and continuousness of man. Faulknerian time is in the most profound and irrefutable sense *human* time. (*Corruption* is that which time brings to the Compsons' lives. *Progress* is the notion of those who are going to make something out of it: "What's in it for me?" ask the Snopeses.) His deepest felt and most often repeated convictions—"They endured." "Man will prevail."—are the long-reached and never-to-be-relinquished resolutions of his passionate idea of human time. And they contain, burned into them, all the plots of Faulkner's novels and stories.

Time, in a novel, may become the subject itself. Mann, attacking the subjectivity of man's knowledge of time, and Proust, discovering a way to make time give back all it has taken, through turning life by way of the memory into art, left masterpieces that are like clocks themselves, giant clocks stationed for always out in the world, sounding for us the high hours of our literature. But from greatest to least, don't most novels reflect that personal subjective time that lived for their writers throughout the writing?

There is the constant evidence of it in a writer's tempo, harmony, the inflections of his work, the symmetry and proportions of the parts in the whole; in the felt rhythms of his prose, his emotion is given its truest and most spontaneous voice; the cadence which is his alone tells us—it would almost do so in spite of him—his belief or disbelief in the story he intends us to hear. But I have in mind something more than this governing of a writer's style.

Faulkner has spoken for the record of his difficulties in writing *The Sound and the Fury*, the novel he loved best and considered his most imperfect; he spoke of its four parts as four attempts, and four failures, to tell his story. In their own degree, many other novels give evidence in themselves of what this difficulty suggests: the novel's duration is in part the measurable amount of time the novelist needs to apprehend and harness what is before him; time is part of the writing too. The novel finished and standing free of him is not the mirror-reflection of that writing-time, but is its equivalent. A novel's duration is, in some respect, exactly how long it takes the particular author of a particular novel to explore its emotional resources, and to give his full powers to learning their scope and meeting their demands, and finding out their truest procedure.

In the very imperfections of *The Sound and the Fury*, which come of a giant effort pushed to its limit and still trying, lies a strength we may set above perfection. They are the human quotient, and honorable as the marks left by the hand-held chisel in bringing the figure out of recalcitrant stone—which is another way of looking at time.

1973

A NOTE ON THE TYPE

The principal text of this Modern Library edition
was set in a digitized version of Janson, a typeface that
dates from about 1690 and was cut by Nicholas Kis,
a Hungarian working in Amsterdam. The original matrices have
survived and are held by the Stempel foundry in Germany.
Hermann Zapf redesigned some of the weights and sizes for
Stempel, basing his revisions on the original design.